STRATEGIES AND STANDARDS FOR DEFENSIVE HANDGUN TRAINING

2023 Edition

Karl Rehn & John Daub

KR TRAINING 512-633-8232
rehn@krtraining.com

www.krtraining.com

Follow us online! Articles, videos and much more!

blog.krtraining.com
www.facebook.com/KRTrainingTexas
https://twitter.com/KRTraining
https://www.instagram.com/krtraining/

Weekly classes Jan-Oct at our Texas facility
check our website for the schedule

We can also bring our training to your location.
Contact us to schedule or
visit the website for remote class information!

To Tom Givens and Massad Ayoob: Friends, mentors and role models in the community of firearms trainers. Your passion, ethics and standards as instructors of armed citizens are the gold standard that inspire us.

Karl: To my wife Penny Riggs, who has been a big part of KR Training for more than 20 years. Co-developer and original co-instructor of many of the courses in our program, designer of the A-Zone range facility and business advisor. KR Training is a thing we built together.

John: To Karl, who took me under his wing over 10 years ago. And to my wife, Michele, who is my reason for doing all that I do.

Acknowledgements

Many thanks to Joan Bowling and Tracy Thronburg for editing large sections of this book. Thanks to Penny Riggs, John Hearne and Jonathan Low for additional input for the April 2019 update. Most, but not all graphics have been updated to include inline references to sources. Thanks to Tess Branson who was our proofreader and formatter for the 2023 edition.

Thanks to Claude Werner, John Correia, John Holschen, John Farnam, Greg Ellifritz, Paul Gomez, Michael Bane, Harel Shapira, Ben Stoeger, David Yamane, John Hearne, Bill Wilson, Ken Hackathorn, John Farnam, Todd Green, Greg Hamilton, Bill Rogers, Brian Enos, Gabe White, Sherman House, and all the other instructors, bloggers, podcasters, and writers mentioned in this book, for your insights and contributions to the field of defensive handgun training.

CONTENTS

ABOUT THE AUTHORS

Karl Rehn has been in the training business since 1991, as training director and lead instructor for KR Training. KR Training's home range, the A-Zone, is an 88-acre training facility in Central Texas. As of March 2023, Karl has attended more than 3,000 hours of formal training from more than 90 different trainers on topics related to firearms and self-defense.

His instructor certifications include National Rifle Association (Training Counselor, all firearm instructor ratings, Advanced Pistol, Practical Pistol Coach), Texas Department of Public Safety (License to Carry Handgun, School Safety, and First Responder instructor), Rangemaster (Basic, Advanced, and Master instructor), Department of Homeland Security (Critical Infrastructure/Risk Protection instructor), Shoot House instructor (Phil Singleton), Deadly Force Instructor (Massad Ayoob Group), Cornered Cat (Kathy Jackson) UTM instructor, pepper spray instructor (Agile Training), Church Security Instructor (Palisades Training), ALERRT Civilian Response to Active Shooter instructor and Simunition® certified instructor.

Prior to retiring from state service and going full time with KR Training, Karl spent 25 years doing research, development and test and evaluation tasks for DoD funded projects at a University of Texas research laboratory. He also spent 10 years developing curriculum, managing instructors, and teaching classes for the Department of Homeland Security, focusing on Critical Infrastructure Protection, Threat Analysis and Risk Mitigation. He also has Masters and Bachelor degrees in Electrical and Computer Engineering from the University of Texas at Austin.

Karl has been a competitive shooter since 1988, primarily in United States Practical Shooting Association (USPSA) and Steel Challenge events. He is currently ranked as Grand Master in five USPSA divisions (Limited, Limited 10, Production, Carry Optics, and Pistol Caliber Carbine), and earned a Master ranking from the International Defensive Pistol Association (IDPA) in the Enhanced Service Pistol division. His shooting accomplishments also include multiple top 5 finishes in the shooting match held as part of each year's Rangemaster Tactical Conference.

KR Training offers training 40+ weeks a year at the A-Zone facility. Most classes are half-day or 1-day courses, from beginner to advanced level, handgun, rifle, shotgun, force on force, medical, legal, and unarmed skills. They also host national level trainers for 2- and 3-day courses many times a year, and offer instructor certification courses from Rangemaster and National Rifle Association, as well as their own Force-on-Force instructor course. KR Training instructors are also available to teach at student locations all over the US. More information is available at www.krtraining.com.

John Daub is senior assistant instructor with KR Training, serving with Karl since 2008. John serves as lead instructor for basic and intermediate level classes, and assisting with all courses. His background includes a wide mix of martial arts, firearms, tactics, legal, and medical training. John is a Rangemaster Certified Master Instructor, Massad Ayoob Group Deadly Force Instructor, Force Science Analyst, NRA Certified Instructor, NRA RSO, Cornered Cat Instructor Development, DTI Instructor development, Agile T&C certified OC Instructor, Image Based Decisional Drills Certified Instructor, Texas DPS Certified LTC Instructor, Texas DPS School Safety trained, Gabe White Light Pin holder, The Complete Combatant purple rank patch, First Person Safety patch, Sig Sauer Certified P365 Armorer, with over 1000 hours of training in firearms, self-defense, emergency medical, unarmed, tactics, vehicle, and other assorted topics in this realm. He also holds a black belt in a semi-useless but sentimental martial art.

John has been a trainer/presenter at the national Rangemaster Tactical Conference. He's been a guest on a number of podcasts including: That Weems Guy, Ballistic Radio, Evolution Security, The ProArms Podcast, The Polite Society Podcast (with Marty Hayes, with Karl Rehn), Handgun World Podcast. He's been referenced in numerous articles and books, including those by Mike Seeklander and Dr. David Yamane.
NRA Benefactor Life Member, TSRA Benefactor Life Member, 2AF Life Member, GOA Life Member, FPC Donor, USPSA Life Member.
In his other life, after 27 years of professional software engineering, architecting, consulting, and directing, John is shifting into the world of information technology (IT) as an architect and consultant. He's also a husband of 25+ years, and father of 3 children. He likes to lift things up and put them down.

FOREWARD to the 1ˢᵗ edition

How can we motivate more people with carry permits, or guns for home defense, to attend training beyond the state minimum?

If the state standards aren't realistic minimum performance standards and don't include all the skills the average gun owner should be trained in, what are those skills and standards?

If you are an instructor of armed citizens, those questions should matter to you. Answer them well, and you can grow your business, offering classes that teach useful information, coaching students to performance standards that might be needed to save their lives.

If you are an armed citizen, these questions matter to you. If you aren't motivated to do more than the state minimum, this book will explain the gap between that minimum and our preferred standards, and the reasons behind those standards. If you are motivated to practice, this book can provide some guidance to a progression of skills and performance standards you can use as a simple training program. If you are motivated to train, this book can help you evaluate the training you've attended and identify gaps or other kinds of classes you may want to explore.

The **Beyond the One Percent** material was originally developed and presented by Karl Rehn at the 2017 Rangemaster Tactical Conference as a four-hour lecture. The Rangemaster Tactical Conference is an annual event put on by Tom Givens and his Rangemaster staff, where dozens of national trainers present short blocks of instruction. It's attended by hundreds of people each year, including national, state and local trainers and their students. The response to this presentation was strong, as the concepts in it began appearing in blogs, podcasts, and magazine articles produced by those who attended. Karl converted the presentation into a multi part series of blog posts and discussed the material on podcasts in 2017 and 2018, and he will be presenting a 2-hour version of this material at the 2019 Rangemaster Tactical Conference.

The **Minimum Competency for Defensive Pistol** material was originally developed and presented by John Daub on his blog between 2013 and 2019. Part of the inspiration for the series was the effort, internal to KR

Training, to develop our own simple, low-round-count shooting test to use in classes. This led to the creation of our Three Seconds or Less test, which tests specific skills, in carefully chosen proportions, to standards meeting our concept of realistic practical minimums for the average armed citizen. In this section, John discusses many different shooting tests and how they compare to our concept of minimum competency.

The **Drills** material comes from a list John and Karl compiled when they guest-hosted an episode of Bob Mayne's Handgun World Podcast on December 24, 2017. The goal was to define a sequence of 10 drills, each of increasing difficulty, testing more skills, to higher proficiency levels, that could define training standards for any defensive handgun shooter. One byproduct of this effort was the assessment of the relative difficulty of many drills, relative to top scores on widely known shooting tests. Karl presented on this topic at the 2014 Rangemaster Tactical Conference, and much of that material is incorporated here. This section of the book will also discuss the design considerations of the KR Training Three Seconds or Less Test in detail.

If you are unfamiliar with any of the drills or targets referenced in this book, more information can be found about them online. Two good places to start are **blog.krtraining.com** and **blog.hsoi.com**, where the original articles and blog posts that inspired this book can be found.

FOREWARD to the 2023 edition

Since the original publication of this book, John and I have continued to think about the topics it addressed, including developing new curriculum in our courses, collecting new data, and creating new shooting drills. We've also presented new material at the annual Rangemaster Training Conferences and discussed our ideas with other trainers and industry experts in person, online, and as guests on podcasts.

The entire book is a collaboration between John and I, but for ease of writing, I presented the information in Section 1, John presented the information in Section 2, and we alternated in our contributions for the final Drill section. We hope you find the information that we present informative, useful, and thought provoking.

Highlights of the new material in this edition include:

- The impact of permitless carry and the elimination of state training requirements on gun owners' interest in training
- The appeal and flaws of popular misconceptions of untrained gun owners new to carrying outside the home
- Deeper insight into the skills and proficiency level related to minimum defensive pistol competency and functional automaticity
- Analysis of relative difficulty of additional popular drills
- Refinements of the list of Top 10 Drills

•

SECTION 1: BEYOND THE ONE PERCENT

Chapter 1
KR Training and Gun Culture 2.0

The history of KR Training parallels the growth of the firearms training industry over the past 20 years. When I, Karl Rehn, started KR Training back in 1991, it was the only firearms training school in the Austin area. No one was offering NRA instructor training, and no one was hosting national-level trainers. Texas did not have state concealed carry permits, and there was no requirement for Hunter Safety training to get a hunting license, so demand for formal classes in how to shoot was basically zero. What motivated me to start offering classes and get certified as an NRA instructor were requests from friends and co-workers. In 1988, I started shooting matches with the local United States Practical Shooting Association (USPSA) club. I had no formal training in handgun shooting when I showed up. A few club members (Randy Johnson, Alan Tillman, and Don Davis) spent time with me helping me get started, and by 1991, with a lot of practice, I was winning local matches and occasionally getting to practice with local legend Chip McCormick as he trained for the Steel Challenge World Speed Shooting Championship. Chip had won the match in 1986 and in 1988. I competed in the 1991 match and finished in the middle of the pack.

Most of my friends and co-workers did not grow up with guns. As my interest in shooting grew, they began asking to go to the range with me to learn. A few of the regular club shooters also asked me to coach them so they could improve. The University of Texas had a program called Informal Classes. It offered short courses on weekdays and evenings on a variety of non-college topics, mostly related to hobbies and sports, and they were always looking for new programs and instructors. That program distributed 50,000 catalogs, embedded in the Austin Chronicle weekly newspaper, all over town, 6 times a year. The UT rifle team coach (back when UT had a rifle team) offered a .22 rifle course through the Informal Classes program, using the indoor range underneath the ROTC building. The range was open many weekday evenings and any graduate of the class could come in and practice whenever they wanted using the rifle club .22 rifles. I took that rifle class and did some additional practice that fall, but I was much more interested in larger caliber handguns.

Search for handgun training in early 1988 is what eventually led me to the USPSA club.

I contacted the Informal Classes program and proposed a class called "Handgun Beyond Basics" – a 4-hour class for people who already knew how to shoot but wanted to shoot better and I arranged to rent a berm at the outdoor range where I practiced multiple days a week to run it. Response to the class was good, and I began offering that course several times a year. After I got certified as a National Rifle Association (NRA) instructor, I started offering an NRA basic pistol class, as well as the Beyond Basics class through the Informal Classes.

In 1993, Ken Humphrey and I created the KR Training website, coding by hand in HTML 1.0, scanning printed photos taken with a film camera, compressing files to tiny sizes so the page would load quickly over dialup access. Back then, Mosaic was the only browser. I was active on USENET newsgroups, promoting my classes anywhere I could. Even back in that era, Austin had a steady flow of people coming to town from California and the east coast, attracted by the growing high-tech industry (Motorola, Apple, IBM, AMD, and many others had major operations there). Multiple universities and colleges in the Austin area had a combined student population of over 60,000 each semester. Between my internet promotion and the print catalogs, I was reaching a lot of potential customers. In many ways KR Training (and its students) were characteristic of what Michael Bane labeled "Gun Culture 2.0."

By 1994, I had begun to realize that I needed more training than I had in how to teach, and in some of the topics I was teaching. That led to a major investment of all my available money and time, traveling to California to get certified as an NRA Training Counselor (able to train and certify other instructors, because there were no Training Counselor certification courses offered in Texas), taking private lessons with several national and world-level shooters in Central Texas (Jim Griggs and Ted Bonnet), and even finding ways to take weekend courses when my day job sent me on the road. A big project that sent me to Seattle area for weeks at a time connected me with NRA trainer Wendell Joost, and then Marty Hayes (Firearms Academy of Seattle) and InSights Training Center (Greg Hamilton and John Holschen). Those businesses were my model for KR Training's expansion: locally based trainers offering a variety of classes and hosting national trainers.

At that time, though, I was only teaching a dozen days a year, spending more time shooting local and major matches and taking classes than teaching them. Demand for training was still low in comparison to what was about to happen. The 1994 "assault weapon" ban grabbed headlines and people who had not been that interested in guns were out buying high capacity magazines and semiauto pistols and rifles. Competition shooting was the subject of every gun magazine; video stores had tapes you could rent showing pro shooters shooting fast and looking cool; and, participation in local matches tripled.

In 1995, Texas passed "shall issue" concealed carry, with a mandatory training requirement. Suddenly everyone wanted to be an NRA instructor, and I was the only active Training Counselor in the area. Demand for NRA instructor training exploded, even after the Texas Department of Public Safety (DPS) decided they would run the License To Carry (LTC) instructor courses themselves and not use the NRA certification. They did exempt those who were NRA certified from the first 2 days of the LTC instructor course. So many found it simpler to attend my weekend 2-day NRA instructor class, pick up that certification and then take a 3 day weekday course at the DPS academy. Fewer days off work and an additional certification was appealing to many.

During KR Training's entire history, I had collected student mailing addresses and email addresses. We started putting out a monthly print newsletter and email updates. The first day that state-certified LTC courses could be offered (September 1, 1995), I had multiple instructors teaching out of a leased office space with 3 classrooms running classes every weeknight and range sessions every weekend for months. Through a combination of being in the right place, at the right time, and a few fortuitous advertising decisions (Informal Classes catalog and internet presence), we found ourselves atop the wave of changes bringing in the Gun Culture 2.0 era.

The number of people offering the state LTC course grew exponentially, and following the basics of economics, class prices (and length) were driven down. We wanted to run the class the maximum 15 hours the state allowed, to cover all the material properly, but had to shift to running the 10 hour "minimum" version at a reduced price. What to do with that other 5 hours of material? Shouldn't people getting certified to carry

Karl Rehn & John Daub

actually learn how to draw from a holster? That topic wasn't covered in the state class at all. In 1998, I married Penny Riggs, a competition rifle shooter from Texas A&M University who had attended one of my NRA instructor classes a few years prior. We stayed in contact after class. When she started teaching LTC classes in College Station, as one of the first active trainers there, the local paper put her on the front page. I shot some high power rifle matches with her, she shot USPSA matches with me, and I proposed one night on the beach after day one of a statewide USPSA match in Corpus Christi, Texas. We were both certified USPSA range officers and believed ourselves capable of teaching other people the basics of holster use. The next evolution of the business began with our decision to start developing and offering our own post–LTC courses.

That decision led us to a long series of "firsts" to our local area. KR Training was already the oldest and largest training business, and the first (only) to offer any courses other than the state mandated class. We were offering basic classes, Beyond the Basics and NRA instructor training. We added to that by hosting national traveling trainers, buying or building enough props to incorporate elements from USPSA matches into our classes (barricades, ports and steel targets), and investing money and time into learning how to run force–on–force training. We eventually developed a one day course that was all scenarios specific to armed citizens, with input from John Holschen of InSights Training, Marty Hayes (Firearms Academy of Seattle), and information from the Simunition® instructor course I took from Ken Murray.

By end of the 1990's, there were hundreds of thousands of people with carry permits in Texas. Everyone was on the internet, and most of our competitors in the LTC training market were people we had probably certified as NRA instructors, who got our monthly newsletter. The market for post–LTC training was large enough to support a small number of those classes each year. A few others began trying to emulate our programs, with lesser success. The range owners of the private facility we had been using to teach our classes encouraged and assisted us in taking the next big step forward: purchasing land and building our own permanent range. After 9/11, it was clear that demand was going to increase again, and I looked at the option of building an indoor range in Austin, leaving my day job with the state to go full time, or buying land outside of town and building an outdoor range facility. The numbers clearly showed the outdoor range option was the best plan. We opened the A-Zone on 02/02/02, after spending fall 2001 and winter 2002 doing most of the labor to complete the classroom building on weekends and over Christmas break.

Fast forward to January 2020. The past 5 to 10 years have seen significant expansion in the number of training schools; in fact, many individuals in my area have started schools similar to mine, including quite a few instructors who have built their instructor resumes by attending courses that I have taught and hosted. New ranges have opened, all offering training classes that are taught by instructors of wildly varying quality, from excellent to unqualified. Someone with no training experience and no credentials, but with enough money or expertise, can create a very professional looking website, creating the impression to the consumer that they are identical, or perhaps superior, to an established business.

These multiple training options, along with the ever-changing metrics Google uses for search engine result placement, change the way people find information online. Additionally, other factors have made it more difficult for KR Training to stand out in a sea of similar-looking websites, Facebook ads, and other marketing strategies. The days of reaching a wide audience with a Yellow Pages ad, a newspaper ad, a radio or TV ad, or even relying on being the top Google search result are over. Most gun owners have little to no understanding of which credentials are hard to get and which are easy beyond "NRA certified" or "former law enforcement" or other vague terms. A recent list of social media "influencers" from the gun industry showed that out of the top 40, less than 5 were trainers or competition shooters with any significant credentials. The remainder, many with followers and subscribers in the millions, may be skilled at making entertaining videos, have levels of fame and name recognition far exceeding some of the most respected trainers with decades of experience and some of the world's best competition shooters. The days where Gun Culture 1.0 people learned who all the good trainers were, and what all the correct techniques were, from articles written by a handful of writers in a small number of print gun magazines are long gone.

The number of people with carry permits is at an all-time peak. The number of guns in private hands is at record levels, as is NRA membership and just about every other indicator related to gun ownership and armed self-defense in the US. Availability of training, much of it competent to excellent, in or near all the major metro areas in the US, is the best it's ever been. But as these numbers show, 99 percent or more of those who could, should, or would benefit from taking training beyond the state minimum either have no interest in it, cannot afford the money or time to attend it, or don't perceive enough value (even pure entertainment value) in it to attend.

Chapter 2
Getting More People To Train

The key question becomes:

How do we get more people to attend training beyond the state minimum?

Since both of my college degrees are in engineering, and after spending 23 years working in military-funded research, development, test and evaluation, I like data. Consequently, my first task in answering the key question was to try to analyze existing data regarding those people who do and do not train and shoot regularly. To identify pertinent data, I formulated specific questions for targeted research:

(1) What is the approximate number of gun owners / carry permit holders?
(2) What is the estimated number of people who train to a mandatory minimum level (state carry permit, hunter education, military, and law enforcement)?
(3) What is the estimated number of people who take at least one class per year or shoot one match per year?
(4) What reasons motivate those people to train and compete?
(5) For what reasons do gun owners not train or compete?
(6) What approaches might motivate a higher percentage to participate?

The Transportation Security Agency (TSA) tracks and reports on firearms discovered at checkpoints. That statistic is interesting because it is tied to the number of people carrying, what guns they are carrying, and how they are carrying them. More people are being caught with guns in their carry-on bags. In fact, between 2015 and 2016, there was a 28% increase. That increased number of guns found in carry-on bags means that more people are carrying guns in their bags and forget the guns are there. Unfortunately, forgetting is reflective of the seriousness (or lack thereof) of their mindset about carrying. Someone serious about carrying would not only remove the gun from the carry-on bag, he or she would also be checking that gun to be able to carry it at his destination, if allowed by local law. According to TSA data, 83% of the guns discovered in carry-on bags are loaded. It is difficult to determine from the TSA data whether "loaded" means a round was chambered or not, but, for sure, I know it means that ammunition was in the gun. This stat implies that most of the people lugging a gun around in their bags were doing so for self-defense reasons.

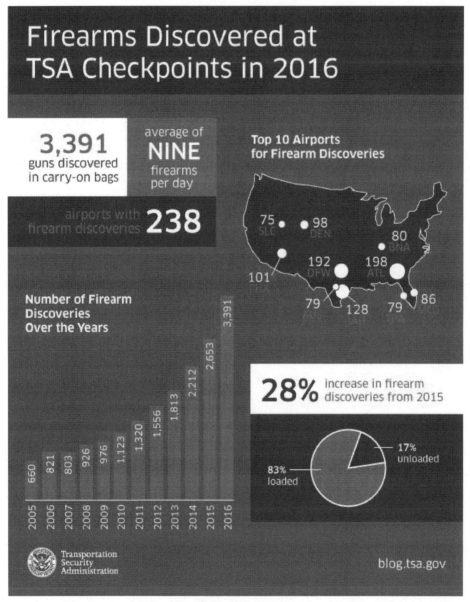

https://www.usatoday.com/story/travel/flights/2016/01/27/tsa-guns-weapons/79362942/

Now for some national numbers, collected from a variety of sources and combined: One of the best sources I found was the National Shooting Sports Foundation (NSSF). The national landscape appears to be this: of the 311 million people in the U.S., 247 million are adults, and 55 million are gun owners. Of that 55 million, NSSF estimates as many as 20 million do some kind of shooting each year. John Lott's data on national concealed carry statistics indicates that there are over 11 million carry permit holders. (The growth of constitutional carry, where no license is required, is going to make an accurate estimate of the number of carry permits more difficult.) The NRA claims 5 million members, about 1/11th of the total pool of gun owners. The NSSF claims that 5 million Americans shoot some type of competition. Whether this statistic covers a lifetime or this year is unclear. I believe that number likely represents the number of gun owners who have ever shot any match of any kind—almost a million cops, 125,000 NRA instructors, and smaller numbers for the competitive pistol sports. *(USPSA and the International Defensive Pistol Association (IDPA) numbers were inferred from press releases and websites.)*

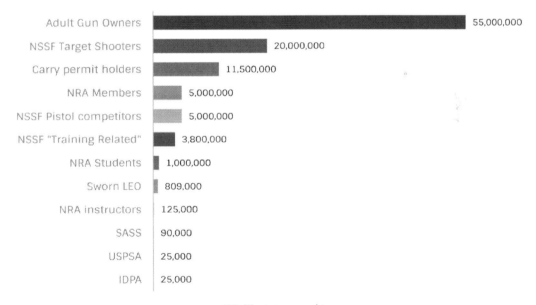

KR Training graphic

My next step was to drill down into the numbers for my home state of Texas, both because it is where my business is located and because Texas has more data available than other states. Our concealed carry license bill required the state police to collect statistics on the number of permits issued, denied, revoked, and other data on crimes committed by permit holders. That data has been very useful to gun politics activists as it makes a strong case for the overwhelming law-abiding nature of carry permit holders. The numbers also show the strength of the gun culture in Texas.

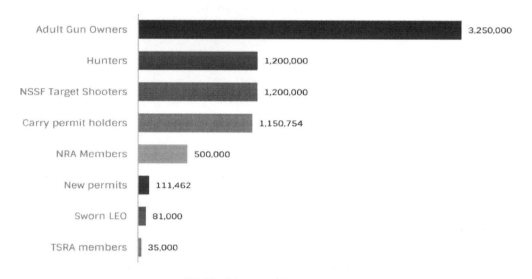

Adult Gun Owners	3,250,000
Hunters	1,200,000
NSSF Target Shooters	1,200,000
Carry permit holders	1,150,754
NRA Members	500,000
New permits	111,462
Sworn LEO	81,000
TSRA members	35,000

KR Training graphic

The Texas population (29 million) is roughly 9% of the national number, but our gun ownership percentage is above average. For simplicity, when no state-level number was available, I used 10% of the national number as an estimate. Based on NSSF and state-level data, there are approximately 3.2 million gun owners in Texas, 1.2 million who buy hunting licenses each year (data provided by Texas Parks and Wildlife), 1.1 million carry permits (from Texas Department of Public Safety), an estimated 500,000 NRA members, with an average of over 100,000 new carry permits issued each year. Sadly, I also learned that membership in the Texas State Rifle Association (TSRA) is only 35,000. Considering that TSRA has played a key role in lobbying for concealed carry and all the improvements in Texas gun laws over the past 30 years, it is shameful that so few Texas gun owners support that organization. Annual membership is less than the cost of 100 rounds of ammo and a range fee for most people, even less for seniors.

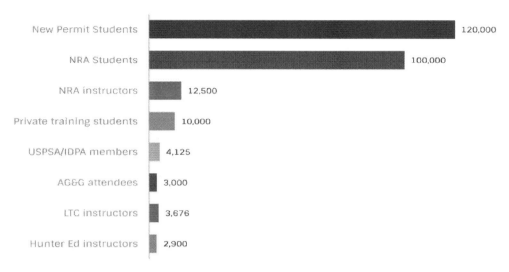

KR Training graphic

Trying to estimate how many actually train or compete each year was difficult. NSSF does not track training as one of their metrics, focusing only on target shooting, hunting and competition. Texas DPS data shows that on average 100,000 people take the new permit course each year, and there are over 4000 LTC instructors. That statistic means that the typical License to Carry (LTC) instructor is teaching fewer than 30 people per year.

The NRA claims to train over 1 million students per year, so 10% of that 1 million is 100,000, taught by the 12,500 (estimated) NRA instructors in the state. That statistic means the typical NRA instructor is teaching 8 people per year. Since NRA classes are not required for the state carry permit, the estimate of 100,000 may be high. Most NRA training conducted in Texas relates to youth programs such as Boy Scouts and 4-H, with some NRA basic pistol courses offered.

Texas has a number of major fixed-location, national-level and state-level schools, including KR Training, that teach classes 30 or more weeks per year. I attempted to estimate the total number of students attending classes at those schools by listing all the schools I know about, asking contacts in major cities all over the state to add names to that list, looking at the calendars on those schools' websites, and asking people I know who had attended those schools what the class sizes were. That marginally scientific approach produced an estimate of 10 schools that taught over 500 students per year and maybe another 20 schools that taught between 100 and 499 students per year, for a rough estimate of 10,000.

On the competition side, I found an NSSF report that provided a statistic on the likely overlap between USPSA and IDPA members, and I used that number to reduce the original estimate of 5,000 (based on national membership numbers claimed in press releases) down to 4,125. There are people who shoot matches that are members of either national organization who were not counted.

The Austin-based organization, A Girl and a Gun (AG&AG), estimated that over 3,000 women participate in at least one AG&AG event in Texas each year. There are other women's shooting groups in Texas, including the Sure Shots, Well Armed Woman, Pistols and Pearls, Shoot Like a Girl, and Second Amendment Sisters. Their participants were not counted in my estimate, as these groups are smaller and, at best, are likely to add less than another 1,000 to the total, particularly since many active in one group are also active in others.

Summarizing the Texas data: 93% of the 3.2 million adult gun owners in Texas likely do not train. Four percent of them take the mandatory new permit course; at best, 3% of them take some kind of NRA course; and only 1%, less than 30,000, take any kind of post-LTC level course or shoot any kind of match, including all kinds of pistol, NRA high power, and all the shotgun sports. If a person takes the LTC class one time that puts him in the 4% category for that year. Those who have not taken a subsequent class are among the 93% all those other years. The same statistic applies for taking a post-LTC class. One who took subsequent class in 2015 was a one-percenter that year, and a ninety-three percenter in 2016.

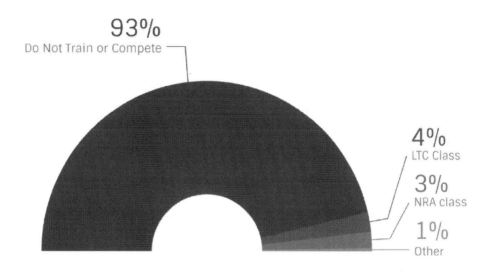

KR Training graphic

NSSF data provides some encouraging results, though. It indicates that in Texas, 22% of the 3.2 million gun owners shoot 5 days or more each year, with 3% shooting more than 20 days per year. It is likely that all the regular competitors and serious shooting school students fall into that 3%, so removing them from the pool means there are maybe 76,000 frequent target shooters who like shooting enough and do it frequently enough that they might be interested in training courses that go beyond the minimum.

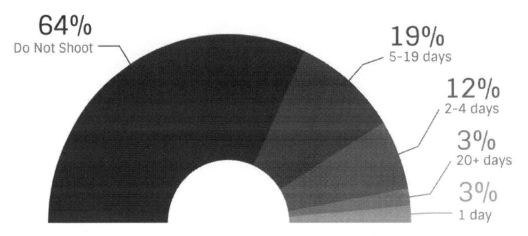

64%
Do Not Shoot

19%
5-19 days

12%
2-4 days

3%
20+ days

3%
1 day

Data: National Shooting Sports Foundation, Sport Shooting Participation in the United States in 2014

This analysis indicates that there are more than 96,000 Texas residents who shoot more than 20 days a year. If you subtract the 10,000 who may take a course once a year, and another 10,000 who are competition shooters in the practical shooting sports, that's another 76,000 people who like to shoot and do it frequently, that are potential students, if they can be reached with the right combination of location, pricing, course length and topic.

Chapter 3
Common Motivators

Having established that a large percentage of people who participate in handgun training do not pursue further training, the next questions become:

What are people's primary motivators?
What motivates shooters?

According to National Shooting Sports Foundation research, people go target shooting for 3 primary reasons:

Camaraderie – 68% (They go with family and friends.)
Sport/recreation – 61%
Self-defense – 59%

The issue that interests me, as someone trying to fill classes that go beyond the state minimum, is this:

Why do people train beyond the state minimum?

Maslow's hierarchy of human needs is a good place to start. Maslow utilizes a pyramid that rests on a base of Physiological Needs and tapers upward through Safety, Belonging, and Esteem to the point of Self-Actualization.

Meeting one or more of these needs drives many of our decisions, both long-term and short-term. If most people had to identify the need they think motivates the majority of people who train beyond the minimum, they would probably guess "Safety." However, that may not be the case. Being a much more profitable, economically larger industry than firearms training, the video game industry has inspired (or funded) more research into understanding what motivates players than gun schools have. Consequently, I looked at some of those studies and some pop culture articles to determine whether their conclusions were applicable to the gun/shooting sports.

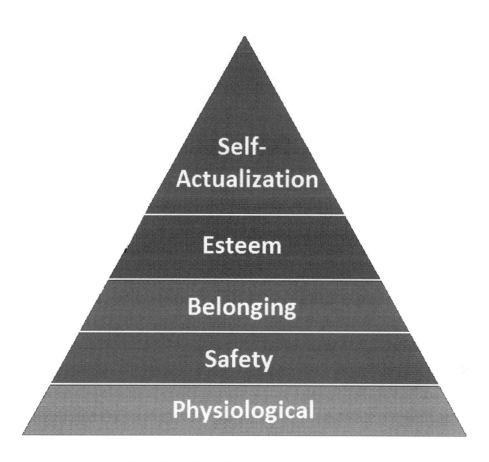

My research reveals the following three main attractions:
Achievement (winning, but also skill development)
Social interaction (in multiplayer games)
Immersion (fantasy fulfillment).

The gun school/competition subculture is also clearly based on these motivators.

Competition shooters want to win their division or the whole match. Those who earn the top tier ratings (Expert, Master, and Grand Master) take pride in those accomplishments. There are schools and specific classes offered by national firearms schools that are known to be hard, with status associated with attaining their Advanced rating or being top shooter in their classes. Some students want to learn every variation of every technique for every task and want to debate the pros and cons of those techniques *ad infinitum* online, usually heaping great scorn upon those who do not use the exact same techniques they use, for the same reasons they chose them. Many just like the challenge of trying to improve their own skills, both the analysis of skills and performance data and the effort involved in improvement, particularly tracking their gains and posting about them to social media.

Shooting well requires a lot of concentration. That is one form of immersion. Taking that step from occasional target shooter to "Serious Student of the Gun" requires an investment of time that can immerse the person in something separate from the mundane annoyances of daily life. The size of the aftermarket upgrade industry for 1911, AR-15, Glock, and other popular guns shows that those who immerse themselves in the gun culture love customizing gear to make it have character that reflects the owner. Additionally, many people have "classtumes" that only get worn to the range, play clothes to go and spend a day in some degree of live-action roleplay. None of those things is inherently bad. My point here is that all those factors appeal to us in various ways, and they bring us pleasure and satisfaction.

The best thing about shooting is that immediate gratification offered by an accurate shot. It makes us feel good. When something makes us feel good, we want to do more of it. When something makes us feel bad, we avoid it. Consequently, a trainer (in any activity) should understand that nothing motivates someone to do more or to work harder than that feeling of success, or more optimally, feeling that sense of flow that comes from performing that task really well with good results.

I believe people's real motivation to attend training beyond the state minimum has a lot more to do with meeting higher-level needs than it does with safety. To steal a term from neural network researchers, it is a "hidden layer." The trainer's curriculum is the input. All of those factors that have nothing to do with actual personal protection are either satisfied (or not) by the experience the student has in a class, the "hidden layer." When the totality of the experience in a course connects with those social and psychological elements, the result is a positive outcome for student and for the instructor, the "output layer." Based on this premise, motivating those who are not currently interested in doing more than the state's minimum may require appealing to higher-level needs as opposed to a fear-based approach that emphasizes safety as the main reason to attend.

In recent years, academic sociologists such as Dr. David Yamane and Dr. Harel Shapira have done excellent work exploring the gun culture from a sociology perspective. Both have attended multiple classes from many schools, interviewing students and instructors. Shapira published a paper in the March 2018 issue of Quantitative Sociology titled "*Learning to Need a Gun*". The paper's abstract states:

> *Millions of Americans feel the need to carry guns with them everywhere they go. They feel this need in their minds as well as in their bodies. Cognitively, they feel their lives are in danger and physically, they feel unease when they are not carrying their guns. In this article, we demonstrate that the practice of carrying guns is constituted by both cognitive schemas about risk and safety, as well as sensory and embodied experiences of comfort, and even pleasure, in holding, shooting, and carrying a gun. As with other social practices, these cognitive schemas and embodied experiences are not innate, but rather learned. Drawing on interviews with 46 people who regularly carry guns, as well as fieldwork at firearms training schools, we examine the process by which people learn the cognitive schemas (how people think about guns) and embodied experiences (how people physically experience guns) associated with the practice of carrying guns.*

His observation is that training can change motivation, and is a form of indoctrination into the "everyday carry" (EDC) lifestyle. It exposes those outside or adjacent to that subculture to a community of people who consider it normal, rational and desirable to carry a concealed firearm everywhere, all the time, for personal defense. Part of each training course includes discussion of mindset and mental preparedness, and the changes many have to make in their outlook and values to become a person who carries daily and aspires to more than state minimum competencies.

Chapter 4
Risk and Training Assessments

Obviously, people attend shooting-related events (such as classes, matches, conferences, and gun shows) for different reasons. I am going to start with an approach that assumes risk reduction (personal safety) is the primary goal. Remember, however, that this assumption is probably incorrect. The new question asks:

How does someone determine which course(s) to take?

From 2007 through 2016, I managed the Infrastructure Protection training program that the Texas A&M Engineering Extension Service (TEEX) taught as part of a larger block of 50+ courses they offer nationally for the Department of Homeland Security (DHS). In addition to managing full time and adjunct instructors teaching over 200 sessions of those courses annually, I was a co-author of the curricula of the four courses in the certification program. The course most relevant to the individual is the MGT-315 Critical Asset Risk Management course, which focuses on protection of a single facility.

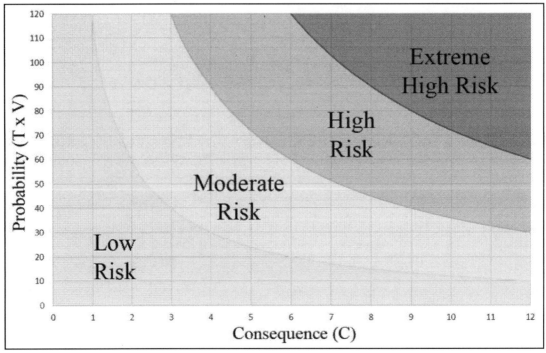

Critical Asset Risk Management (MGT-315), Texas Engineering Extension Service, 2017

The course utilizes the adjacent risk assessment graph, which plots probability (threat x vulnerability) vs. consequences. It considers both the odds and the stakes. To reduce total overall risk, one must identify which risks are highest and then explore options to reduce those risks by lowering the threat, the vulnerability, or the consequences.

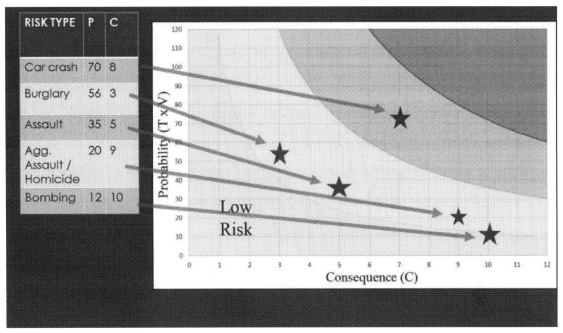

RISK TYPE	P	C
Car crash	70	8
Burglary	56	3
Assault	35	5
Agg. Assault / Homicide	20	9
Bombing	12	10

Critical Asset Risk Management (MGT-315), Texas Engineering Extension Service, 2017

For example, consider the typical armed citizen's risks. Based on statistics, an auto accident is the most likely risk, followed by burglary, assault, aggravated assault/homicide, and bombing. The process for determining values is relatively unscientific. If each individual assigns the risks a consistent value, calibrated by statistics for his personal geographic area and lifestyle, one person's numbers will likely be different from another's. My personal values map to the locations shown on the graph to the right. Some are medium probability, medium consequences. Others, like the bombing risk, are low probability but higher consequence.

RISK TYPE	RISK = T x V x C	LEVEL	
Car crash	560	HIGH	MITIGATE
Burglary	168	MODERATE	
Assault	135	MODERATE	TRANSFER
Agg. Assault / Homicide	180	MODERATE	ACCEPT
Bombing	120	LOW	

Critical Asset Risk Management (MGT-315), Texas Engineering Extension Service, 2017

There are three basic choices to reduce risk: mitigate (do something about it); transfer (make someone else responsible for it); or accept (live with it). Mitigation options include changes to plans, policies, equipment, training, and organization. Transfer options include insurance and outsourcing—depending upon the police/fire/EMS for protection or, within families, depending on a spouse/brother/other relative who trains and always carries, i.e., "I don't need to protect myself since they will protect me". Acceptance speaks for itself.

A longer list of all-hazards risks and the priority areas for action looks like this: Health and fitness are #1. No one in the health and fitness industry has figured out the magic way to motivate everyone to do the right things in those areas. Personally, I am as guilty as anyone of finding reasons not to go get sweaty and of finding opportunities to eat delicious foods that contribute to weight gain. I have taken over 2,500 hours of firearms training and a few hundred hours of medical training. So far in my life, I have needed the medical training more times than I have needed the firearms training.

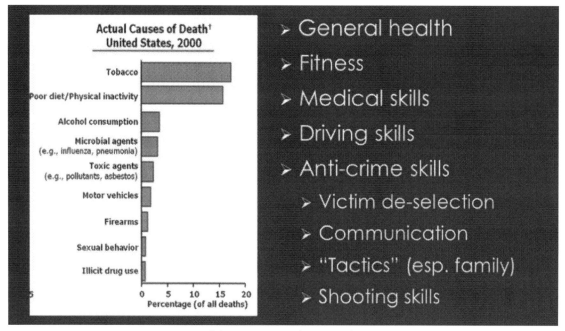

Data: https://www.csdp.org/research/1238.pdf

I drive every day. Being a better driver—not just safer, but better—particularly at accident avoidance, is important. Texas Engineering Extension Service (TEEX) offers a Traffic Accident Avoidance course, using the driving track at the law enforcement academy that includes hands-on training. As an employee, I was able to take the course. Facilities for this type of training are much harder to find than shooting ranges, and classes offering hands-on instruction are difficult to find. Anyone who has access to this type of training should consider attending because better is a large component of safer.

Breaking the category of anti-crime skills into priority order, awareness, communication skills, and non-fighting skills, ranks higher than more assertive skills. In other words, diffuse the situation if possible. However, specific scenarios exist which might require preparation or training. For example, extended loss of power could encourage home invasions; being stranded on the roadside could communicate vulnerability; cyber-attack (identity or financial) could pose a significant risk. In extreme circumstances, pepper spray or defensive gun use may be the only viable line of defense. Interestingly, defensive gun use is not high on the list of anti-crime skills. One way for an individual to compile a list like this is to start with a list of things that he or she has to deal with every year, every five years, every 10 years, and so on. Other scenarios that could require anti-crime skills of some kind might include natural hazard damage to the community, which can lead to food and water shortages, an active shooter situation, urban unrest, a terrorist attack, or civil war. Over the past five years, KR Training has integrated broader preparedness training into our program, first with medical classes from Lone Star Medics and, more recently, through hosting preparedness conferences and seminars. KR Training's Paul Martin presented on Events Other than Violence at the 2017 Rangemaster Tactical Conference in an effort to encourage other firearm trainers to expand their programs in similar fashion.

While gun grappling and ground-fighting are popular areas of study within the private sector training community, review of actual armed citizen incidents (by Claude Werner, in his review of NRA Armed Citizen accounts, and the hundreds of videos available on the Active Self Protection YouTube channel) does not show the likelihood of the need for those skills to be high, compared to basic draw and shoot capabilities. I have taken Craig Douglas's Extreme Close Quarters Concepts class three times and hosted it five times; additionally, I have trained in that topic with Cecil Burch, Insights Training Center (Greg Hamilton/John Holschen), John Benner (Tactical Defense Institute), Tony Blauer, Leslie Buck, and a few others. The training is useful, particularly in developing mental toughness and ability to function under both physical and psychological stress. Clearly, those courses have serious value, but a shooter should keep their value in perspective relative to total risk.

I reviewed Claude Werner's list of Negative Outcomes that frequently occur to armed citizens, and then I paired them with the best solution to reducing them. My findings are shown in the adjacent chart. Scenario-based force-on-force training, not just Simunition® fight club/gunfight classes but even simple red gun roleplay and video simulators, develop skills that are not usually emphasized or, often, are even included in typical live fire classes.

ERROR	BEST SOLUTION
Negligent Discharge	Live Fire Skill
Lacking confidence in ability	Live Fire Skill
Missing / hitting bystander	Live Fire Skill
Shooting w/ no target ID	Scenario / FoF
Chasing criminals	Scenario/ FoF
Unjustified shooting	Scenario/ FoF
Warning shots	Scenario/ FoF
Carrying where illegal	Gun Laws

KR Training graphic

Does training really matter? Gun politics activists who lobby for reduction in (or elimination of) mandatory state training for carry permits have strong arguments and data showing that simply having a gun when one is needed is the most important component. Rarely do examples of an armed citizen's failing due to a slow draw or poor marksmanship occur; much more commonly, failures occur due to errors in judgment and negligence in gun handling.

For someone who goes through life and never needs a gun or the skills that go with it, these statements are not important. Perception of the need for skills affects motivation to train and selection of courses to attend. Often, until a person thinks something is broken, there is no motivation to fix it. For example, I ignored several years of weight gain until it caused back problems and daily back pain in early 2016. Pain moved extra weight from low risk to high priority, motivating me to make changes in diet and exercise and lose 50 pounds.

Everyone knows someone who has a carry permit but never carries or only carries in the car. That person's perception of risk is different from the perceptions of those who carry daily, and both are different from the risk perception of those who carry daily and train seriously. Generally, people carry because they believe they may, at some point, face a violent attacker. Conversely, people tend not to carry because they believe that accidents, failures, loss, injuries, or deaths are rare occurrences, and they tend to ignore or reject information that does not agree with their existing opinions. Moreover, while successful attacks are widely reported, foiled attempts receive little public attention.

Specific to the topic of firearms training, at least 75% of the time, a handgun is going to be used when a firearm is needed in a defensive incident, as opposed to a shotgun or rifle. Based on which of the KR Training courses are most popular, which courses are discussed most frequently by forums or on broadcasts, and information on what courses other schools offer, priorities are somewhat upside down. When one compares trainings that are most valuable to the typical armed citizen to the courses that are most popular, most valuable ranks below popularity.

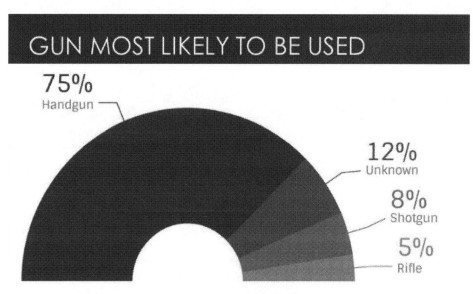

GUN MOST LIKELY TO BE USED

75%
Handgun

12%
Unknown

8%
Shotgun

5%
Rifle

Firearm Justifiable Homicides and Non-Fatal Self Defense Gun Use, Violence Policy Center, June 2015

Classes generally fall into the following categories: state carry permit class; "operator" carbine course; high round count pistol course; team tactics/vehicle course; basic pistol course; defensive long gun course; gun grappling course. **Basic pistol training** ranks Very High. A high-quality basic pistol course is the most important because it builds the fundamentals of safe gun handling and shooting skills that are the absolute most likely to prevent negligent discharges and result in acceptable hits in defensive gun uses. The **state carry permit** ranks High because it is the most needed, not because the content is useful, but because the class is required to be able to carry. The **high round count pistol course** also ranks High in usefulness. **Long gun courses** that are more focused on home and building defense (including carbine and shotgun courses together) rank higher than "enterTrainment" classes. All classes except the basic pistol course are live fire courses, with the **operator carbine course**, which is taken with a chest rig and dump pouch, multicam and so on, being the most popular but the least likely to be needed. Every year, KR Training offers a pocket gun/small gun class that garners an anemic response compared to similar offerings that allow students to use

holsters and guns that they admit they never carry. Participation in divisions in IDPA identify that use smaller guns is low compared to those allowing customized duty-sized guns. Admittedly, shooting a carbine at a 7-yard target is more fun than sitting in classes most of the day and shooting little or not at all, but those less popular classes are more likely to be useful. One big problem in the industry is that there are a lot of people teaching those lower level courses who stopped their own training at the minimum required for certification to teach at that level, leaving a big gap between those courses and the generic 2-day defensive pistol course that national-level traveling trainers offer.

CLASS TYPE (high to low popularity)	LIKELY NEED
State carry permit class	High*
"Operator" carbine course	Very low
High Round Count pistol course	High
Team tactics/vehicle course	Low
Basic pistol course	Very High
Defensive Long Gun course	Low
"Gun grappling" course	Low

CLASS TYPE (low to lowest popularity)	LIKELY NEED
Low light shooting	Low
Scenario Force on Force	Very High
Medical skills course	Very High
Unarmed defense	Very High
Pocket gun class	High
Precision rifle course	Very low
No live fire tactics course	Very High

Just as with diet and exercise, it appears that making the right choices in gun training is hard. Junk food is more pleasurable than health food. The Inconvenient Truth about the private sector training industry is most likely that **actual risk reduction has almost nothing to do with class selection.** Other trainers who offer a variety of courses have observed similar trends in course popularity. Most attempt some balance between offering the courses that always fill and the courses they wish were more popular.

Chapter 5
Standards and Competence

KR Training assistant instructor Tom Hogel once said that he has never had a beginner ask him any of the following important questions:

What classes do I need to take?
What minimum level of competence do I need to have reasonable odds of surviving a deadly force incident?
What do I need to know to be ready for the legal and psychological aftermath?

Clearly, as I have previously established, motivation is not often based on an assessment of need as much as on less obvious psychological factors. The next question, then, becomes:

How can trainers successfully encourage gun owners to not accept mediocrity in their personal skill levels?

Perspectives change as students progress in their training. But the above questions are rarely asked of us by those in basic, license to carry, and even the first level defensive pistol course. Too many gun owners and most with carry permits have an "I shoot well enough" attitude about their readiness for a defensive gun use. Everyone who carries regularly believes their skill level is "good enough," based on one of two definitions: the minimum for their state license, or however well they shoot. Neither of those standards is based on analysis of incidents or the recommendations of trainers who teach more than the state minimum course. There is no shortage of standards and drills available online that someone can use to evaluate his or her skills. Most of these online evaluations, however, require skills that cannot be performed at many ranges: drawing, firing faster than one shot per second, movement. Running the required drills usually necessitates a shot timer, which used to be a big hurdle in that it required buying a $100 gadget. The cost factor is no longer an excuse, since there are shot timer apps for IOS and Android, and many drills are run using par times, which can be done with a stopwatch app. Excuses aside, the real reasons people do not include measurement of skill using standards in practice are not range limitations or gear limitations. The reality is that shooting standards are like taking tests, and nobody likes taking tests, particularly tests for which one feels unprepared or on which one expects to do poorly.

Advocates of Constitutional Carry frequently point out that it is rare, almost unheard of, to find an example in which an armed citizen had a negative outcome as a result of being too slow getting the gun from holster (or drawer, or purse, wherever), aiming at the target, and firing. Similarly, failure to achieve effective hits is rarely the cause of a negative outcome: simply being threatened with deadly force or being shot at and hit anywhere stops the attack much of the time. So are untrained shooters really that big of an issue? Absolutely! In 2014-2015, KR Training ran 118 shooters through a series of shooting tests using iron sights, green lasers, and slide-mounted red dot sights (with and without backup irons). Though I presented the results at the 2016 Rangemaster Tactical Conference, formal publication of the university-funded study is still slowly winding its way through campus review. One result is relevant here. We had 118 shooters, of skill levels from novices to instructor level, shoot a one round test.

The test was simply one shot on target in 1.5 seconds, starting from a ready position and using an International Defensive Pistol Association (IDPA) target at 5 and 10 yards. That shot is somewhat more difficult than the one shot in two seconds at three yards required by the Texas license to carry course, but as the data shows, most of the shooters that were at LTC (License To Carry) level or higher had no trouble getting 0-ring hits.

	NOVICE	LTC	POST-LTC	INSTRUCTOR
5 yard (irons)	88.2%	96.5%	98.9%	99.5%
10 yard (irons)	75.0%	91.9%	97.8%	99.0%

http://blog.krtraining.com/red-dot-study-key-points/

Past the carry permit level, additional training did not make a big difference in that skill. Had we decreased the time limit down to 1.25 or 1 second, we likely would have seen worse performance relative to training level. Training increases speed.

Where training (and more importantly, frequent dry-fire practice) really makes a difference is in the speed of drawing from concealment, a parameter we did not measure in this test. One of the biggest benefits of training is improved gun handling. The level of gun handling considered acceptable at most gun shops, gun shows, commercial ranges, and other places where untrained/LTC-level trained gun owners shoot is lower than what is expected at most post-LTC level courses. Meeting that higher standard significantly decreases the likelihood that a muzzle will be in an unsafe direction or that a finger will be on trigger when it really should not be.

The real value of training, though, is that it improves competence, which leads to a higher level of confidence. Greater confidence leads to more frequent carrying as the student begins to believe in his/her ability to carry in public safely and make legally defensible and tactically correct use-of-force decisions. Training and the resultant confidence can reduce many of the negative outcomes that can occur: failure to engage; gun accidents; legal consequences of poor defensive decisions; or injury or death due to lack of speed or ineffective hits. The biggest problem goes back to that "I shoot well enough" attitude. Until the negative outcome happens, most gun owners will insist that their gun handling is safe enough. And many who could not pass a baseline defensive handgun skills test like KR Training's Three Seconds or Less drill, carry in public with great (un-tested, un-validated) confidence in their skills.

Karl Rehn & John Daub

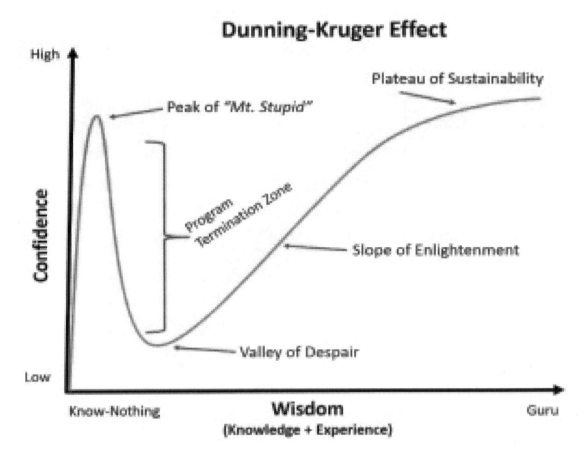

https://xonitek.com/lessons-from-mt-stupid/

This "safe enough" attitude is called the Dunning–Kruger effect. The 99% of carry permit holders, the ones who will not come to a training course that goes beyond the state minimum, are usually at the top of Mt. Stupid. They are not stupid, though. I think many of them do not want to take the next step because they see the giant cliff that lies beyond it. The cliff, marked as the Program Termination Zone, is not a happy place because it is filled with uncertainty and doubt. Once someone becomes aware that his or her skills are not at the level they should be, he or she loses confidence and enters the Valley of Despair.

If a shooter cannot be motivated to go shoot a match or take a class, the issue of denial in defense of the ego may be involved. As Dr. William Aprill has noted, the desire to protect the ego (against poor performance in front of others) often overrides the desire to gain the larger benefit, which is improvement in survival odds. That desire to seek out those activities that have a higher probability of success (carbine courses with 7-yard targets), vs. those activities which may be more challenging (force-on-force scenarios or unarmed courses for the non-martial artist), is definitely a factor in class selection. A good post-LTC training course will get students past the Valley of Despair and move them to the Slope of Enlightenment, where confidence begins to return. Regaining conscious confidence, ascending the Slope of Enlightenment, will require effort: training and practice time. Going from unconscious incompetence to conscious incompetence is not fun.

Hopefully, we all have noble motives. Turning interest into action is more difficult. Anytime I am having a conversation with someone about my training business or receive a contact from someone who tries to coordinate a group class, the divide between being interested enough to say they might go and being willing to commit a deposit and schedule a specific date is wide. Many never get past the "I should do that someday" step.

On one of the social media forums in which I participate, my standard response to the question, "What kind of new gun should I buy?" is to suggest that the questioner spend money on training, range time, and practice ammo with the gun he or she already has, or at least on spare mags, better sights, and good quality carry gear for the gun he or she carries most often. That response is never well received. A sizable chunk of the armed citizen community will spend $500, $1000, or more on a new gun but will not spend one dollar on training. Moreover, the new gun they wanted will spend 364 days a year in the safe alongside all the other new guns that were also briefly interesting. In reality, amateurs think only of equipment. John Holschen (West Coast Armory) has been in the training business for more than 30 years. His analysis matches my own experiences as a student and as a trainer.

Amateurs think equipment,
Students think techniques,
Experts think tactics.
  -John Holschen

Students coming to training just past the carry permit level are interested in techniques. After techniques can be executed with competence, then concerns about tactics follow. Many bloggers have observed that gun reviews are the most popular articles on their sites. Greg Ellifritz publishes the Active Response Training blog, and he observes:

> *The focus of my writing is definitely on software, rather than hardware I've published 1477 articles on my website. Of those 1477 posts, only 53 of them are gun or gear reviews. Even though the equipment articles are a small percentage of my writing as a whole, those posts consistently get the most attention. When I look at the most popular articles on the site, hardware articles make up 10 out of the top 20 most popular posts despite being only 3% of my total material. I have six articles that have been read more than 250K times. Five of those six articles are gun and gear reviews.*

A popular activity online among those with higher levels of training is to criticize the gear used by the less trained, particularly with regard to guns, holsters, and carry methods. Most of the time, that criticism is valid, but it is very poorly received by those with the bad gear. Choosing bad gear based on poor assessment of equipment needs is not unique to the gun culture, as noted in Katherine Burson's paper.

To summarize the bad news, most gun owners do not train past the minimal standards of the mandatory state courses. Many gun owners practice with poorly selected gear (if they practice at all), but they do not attend training. Only 1% to 2% train or participate in competition shooting. For most, the primary goal is recreation, not competence or safety. Telling someone what he or she needs to do is a poor motivator. For those of us trying to offer classes that take gun owners past the state minimum to a realistic level of competence, these hurdles must be overcome to reach more than the one percent.

Chapter 6
Culture Can Change

Culture can and does change. It has changed in many ways since I first became seriously interested in handgun shooting back in 1988. Thus, the new question presents:

How has the shooting culture changed in the last 50 years, and how should trainers adapt to the cultural changes?

A great example on cultural change is the adjacent data on willingness to use a gun in self-defense. The highest numbers on the chart are for women against a male aggressor. That statistic reflects a change from what was the conventional wisdom that women are less likely to use deadly force in self-defense.

Table I. Means for Perceived Danger and Willingness to Use a Gun in Scenarios

| | Female respondent | | | | Male respondent | | | |
| | Female aggressor | | Male aggressor | | Female aggressor | | Male aggressor | |
	Mean	SD	Mean	SD	Mean	SD	Mean	SD
Danger[a]								
Scenario:								
Movie theater	26.91	5.25	29.62	4.38	19.36	6.40	24.12	6.05
Shopping mall	25.41	6.28	30.89	4.52	19.29	7.20	24.89	5.89
Deserted street	24.50	6.34	28.22	5.13	20.21	7.04	23.74	6.07
Convenience store	22.92	9.61	25.50	8.32	19.59	9.25	22.33	8.46
Willingness to use a gun[b]								
Scenario:								
Movie theater	5.41	3.43	6.31	3.39	4.79	3.31	6.33	3.37
Shopping mall	5.15	3.41	7.23	3.97	5.19	3.27	6.31	3.47
Deserted street	5.06	3.10	6.19	3.81	5.24	3.39	6.28	3.68
Convenience store	5.29	3.78	4.79	3.23	5.52	3.76	5.90	3.95

[a]Higher scores indicate greater perceived danger.
[b]Higher scores indicate greater willingness to use a gun.

Gender and Perceptions of Danger, Mary Harris and Kari Miller, Sex Roles, Vol 43, Nos 11/12, 2000

There has been steady growth and cultural change related to women and guns over the past 20 to 30 years. In the 1990s the NRA's "Refuse to be a Victim" program started as a women's-only course and expanded to a wider audience. The Babes with Bullets program paired the top female United States Practical Shooting Association competitors of the day with other women who were either active competitors or were interested in competition. Women and Guns magazine started in the 1990s and is still being published, outlasting other mass market gun publications. The Second Amendment Sisters organization shut down in 2015, but it was very active in the 2000s, promoting the idea of gun rights (and armed self-defense) to women. The larger cultural changes of the mainstreaming of concealed carry and AR-15 ownership increased the appeal of shooting to a more urban and self-defense-oriented audience. In the 2010s, particularly in Texas, growth of women-oriented shooting clubs like A Girl and a Gun, Sure Shots, Pistols and Pearls and many others has been significant.

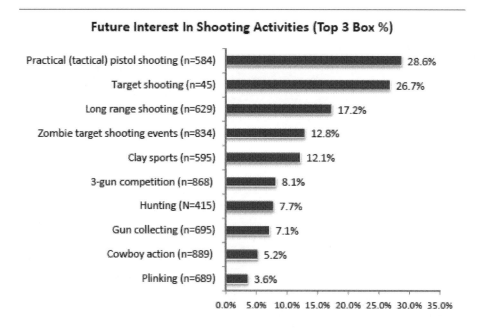

Future Interest In Shooting Activities (Top 3 Box %)

Practical (tactical) pistol shooting (n=584)	28.6%
Target shooting (n=45)	26.7%
Long range shooting (n=629)	17.2%
Zombie target shooting events (n=834)	12.8%
Clay sports (n=595)	12.1%
3-gun competition (n=868)	8.1%
Hunting (N=415)	7.7%
Gun collecting (n=695)	7.1%
Cowboy action (n=889)	5.2%
Plinking (n=689)	3.6%

0.0% 5.0% 10.0% 15.0% 20.0% 25.0% 30.0% 35.0%

From "Women Gun Owners" study, National Shooting Sports Foundation, 2014, pg. 30

Women may present a different training attitude, particularly those who are Gun Culture 2.0 people. These women were not raised around firearms, and they initiate an interest in firearms from outside the gun culture. They are likely to seek out training, often provided by the women-oriented or women-only clubs. The carry permit (and self-defense) remains a key motivator, and, according to an NSSF report on women gun owners, 42% have a carry permit. While 73% take at least one class, they average taking 3.5 classes. Unfortunately, the professionals who teach these courses at the club level are often barely qualified—NRA basic pistol instructor level, state carry permit level, or similar part time/volunteer level. The important trend is that within that subculture, the idea of attending a course is more common than with gun owners in general. NSSF survey data of national A Girl and A Gun members showed interest in activities at higher levels and with different priorities than the data indicated for all gun owners. Simply stated, women take more classes. And women plan to take more classes in the future.

From "Women Gun Owners" study, National Shooting Sports Foundation, 2014, pg. 33

Other cultural changes have occurred over the past 50 years. In the 1970s, all of the gun magazines were about hunting and gun collecting, for the most part. NRA training was all about target shooting and bullseye competition. In the 1980s, concealed carry and USPSA competition started to grow, to the level that a national network shooting show featured USPSA, Steel Challenge, and other modern pistol sports. American Shooter (now called Shooting USA) was reaching a national audience. In the 1990s, significant expansion in concealed carry laws occurred. The political drama over the assault weapon and high capacity magazine ban ironically caused a lot of gun owners who had previously shown no interest in those guns to take an interest and purchase them. Growth of the shooting sports continued, as IDPA started and began to attract gun owners who were interested in USPSA-style shooting but had a more concealed carry focus. The idea that people needed to attend training to be prepared to carry in public and to be proficient with carry guns really took root during this decade.

The attacks on the U.S. that occurred on September 11, 2001dramatically changed the country's risk perception. Suddenly, everyone realized that something bad could happen to them and that they needed to do something about it. Growth of the internet and increased access to information produced by and about gun owners provided a more realistic view than did the consistently anti-gun editorial bias of the mainstream media. Moreover, the information began to be available and accessible to a broader audience. The growth of realistic war and shooting video games increased interest in real firearms as well. The resulting impact of modern communication capabilities was the rise of Gun Culture 2.0, a term coined in 2012 by gun writer, competition shooter, and TV producer Michael Bane to describe the 2000s' trends.

The 2010s brought tremendous growth in sales and demand for training, in response to concerns that President Obama would enact a variety of gun bans and new restrictions (particularly after the shooting at Sandy Hook elementary school in 2013). After decades of refusing to consider the idea of training civilians to draw from a holster (while lobbying in every state to get concealed carry laws passed), the NRA finally published its **Personal Protection Outside the Home** course and began certifying its own instructors to teach the same skills the private sector had been teaching since the 1970s. By this time, gun magazines (and online content) had shifted completely from hunting and bullseye shooting to nothing but practical, action, defensive-oriented, high speed, run-and-gun content. The NRA magazines began covering 3-gun, a real change in focus for them. In 2019, the NRA introduced a modular Concealed Carry class that allows instructors to build a course using one or more modules, to meet state requirements or the needs of pre- and post-carry permit level students.

Back in the 1990s our local IPSC club attempted to build a private range and was sued by adjoining landowners. The NRA sent a Range Design representative to help us, but he had no pistol experience and had never seen a USPSA match. The idea that people could draw loaded guns from holsters, shoot in directions other than straight ahead down their tiny assigned firing point, and move while shooting was completely outside his comfort zone, and was too "extreme" for NRA HQ to support. As culture has changed, the NRA's positions have changed, sometimes with the natural lag and resistance to change inherent in any large organization.

Sociologist Dr. David Yamane studied the ad content in the NRA magazines over a 100 year period. His data show the shift from a hunting and target shooting focus to defensive training and action-oriented competition over that time.

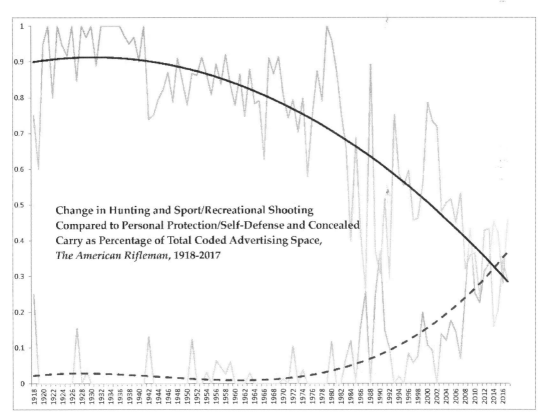

Change in Hunting and Sport/Recreational Shooting Compared to Personal Protection/Self-Defense and Concealed Carry as Percentage of Total Coded Advertising Space, *The American Rifleman, 1918-2017*

"The Rise of Self-Defense in Gun Advertising: The American Rifleman, 1918-2017," in Gun Studies, David Yamane, Sebastian L. Ivory, and Paul Yamane, 2017

Just because a large percentage of existing gun owners have not embraced the need or value, and fun, in competing or training, that statistic does not mean those numbers will remain at those low levels. In 1992, the number of gun owners interested in the AR-15 was tiny. In 2019, the AR-15 is the most commonly purchased rifle. The same trend is evident for the numbers of people with carry permits and the numbers of people who carry daily. The trends are positive for the future of both training and practical/defensive type competition, if for no other reason than the increased numbers of gun owners. If only 1% attend training, 1% of the pool of gun owners today is a larger number than it was 10 years ago or 20 years ago.

However, culture change does not occur on its own. The messages people hear and the examples high profile people set affect opinion and behavior. Sometimes, ideas that start in a quiet corner spread quickly because they are the right idea at the right time. At this point in history, a lot of voices exist on many different platforms, all being heard by gun owners and pro-gun voters. Clearly, the potential exists to affect the gun owner opinions that influence their decisions to attend training.

Chapter 7
Permitless Carry and Training

As of February 2023, twenty-five states now allow permitless carry. In most of those states, it is still possible to get a carry permit, and often the carry permit provides additional benefits. For example, after permitless carry passed in Texas, many businesses that previously allowed concealed carry posted "30.05" signs, which prohibit unlicensed carry. Often they were posted alongside the "30.07" (no open carry) signs.

Instructors whose primary business relied on teaching state-mandated classes haven't been happy about this change. The most commonly taught state mandated course was the NRA Basic Pistol class. It covers shooting fundamentals, safe handling and storage, but does not teach proper, safe use of a holster, tactics, or use of force law. The Texas course does teach use of force law, but many students misinterpret what is taught. Use of force really falls into 3 categories: Can, Should and Must. State law defines the outer box: the boundaries of when you *can* shoot. Those that choose to shoot in those situations often end up going to trial. I've worked many cases as an expert witness for armed citizens that used deadly force since 2018, and by far the most common problem is choosing to act in situations where the "Can" criteria may be met, but the "Should" and "Must" have not. In those situations, they had other options available. KR Training students that have been in similar situations who used other actions: verbal, pepper spray, physical force, leaving the scene, or display of a firearm without firing, have not been arrested or charged.

Nothing in the curriculum for the Texas carry permit course, nor the NRA Basic Pistol course, really emphasizes the importance of Can/Should/Must. Texas, like many other states, currently has big problems with guns being stolen from vehicles. In Sept 2022, the Houston Chronicle reported that over 4,000 guns had been stolen from parked cars. In January 2023, there were multiple car burglaries on our block in Bryan, Texas. Local PD were knocking on doors on our block urging people that had guns in vehicles to bring them indoors. During a recent drive from Baton Rouge back to Bryan, I saw multiple billboards posted by the state of Louisiana urging residents to stop leaving guns unsecured in vehicles. Yet this practice remains popular and common, exacerbated by the recent popularity of "holster magnets" and other gadgets designed to facilitate a quick draw from the driver's seat of a vehicle.

One expert witness case I worked in early 2023 involved one of these devices. The untrained person concerned about carjacking envisions a scenario in which someone is at their car window, probably waving a gun, wanting them to get out and give them the car and/or their money. In the untrained person's mind, the best solution is to draw against a pointed gun and get into a 1 yard shootout. When we run those simulations in force on force classes, the driver never survives.

As we explain in classes, wearing the gun concealed (not leaving it exposed for someone standing at the car window to see) gives you the option to bail out of the car, armed, without the attacker knowing. That provides many options up to and including waiting to draw and engage until the attacker is preoccupied getting into the car. At a minimum keeping the gun out of sight prevents the attacker from seeing the gun and opening fire before you can even grab it. Worse, those that choose to "carry in the car" rarely (never?) have a holster in the vehicle. So even if they wanted to carry the gun on-body outside the vehicle, their only option is to stuff the gun in their pants the way criminals do. Those that suffer from "carry in the car" often insist that carrying on body is just "too hard", usually based on an hour's time spent carrying in a low budget holster purchased at a big box retail store.

The car shootout fantasy can obscure consideration of other options, for example driving away. In the 2023 case (which was actually an incident that occurred Jan 2020 that took 3 years to get to trial), the driver had pulled into a gas station, followed by the road rage driver. The road rage driver jumped out of his car and ran over to the client's car. The client's car was still running, and was in D, with his foot on the gas. Instead of driving away, the client chose to try to talk to the road rage driver through his open window. The road rage driver responded by punching the client, who grabbed his pistol from its steering column-attached holster and shot the road rage driver twice.

Even though the client immediately began doing CPR on the person he shot, and even though the client gave a quality statement to the police (without an attorney present, however) after the incident, in a small Texas town he was still prosecuted, and ended up accepting a plea deal for a felony charge.

In another road rage case that I was consulted on, another driver had his gun stuck between the seats on his right side, for quick access. When he encountered a problem, his first response was to draw and fire at the armed person outside the window. His case has not yet gone to trial, but it's in anti-gun jurisdiction, and all the witnesses believe that his actions were unjustified.

The root problem here is that the gun accessory "industry" makes a product that appeals to the poorly thought-out tactics choices. They are engaging in recognition primed decision making: programming themselves that draw and shoot is the best immediate response to a variety of vehicle-based situations – even though specialists in vehicle tactics courses teach otherwise. In the vehicle tactics classes I've attended, driving away, if the car is mobile, is always recommended. When I have brought this point up with untrained gun owners on internet forums, their pushback is substantial. They will insist that the experts I cite are wrong and the cases I've worked are anomalies, exhibiting serious Dunning-Kruger behaviour. Most of these people are graduates of a Texas carry permit course or other mandated training from other states.

Because of this and many other experiences, I do not mourn the days of state-mandated classes, as I simply haven't seen that the training produces any actual benefit. The change that we have seen is that fewer people taking state mandatory classes has not led to an increase in people seeking non-mandatory training. Those motivated to train beyond state minimums still do so; those that never believed they needed any training in the first place, who were unlikely to change their opinions or behaviour as a result of a state mandated course, are happy about the change. Those that lacked the funds or the time to jump through the state hoops, but are motivated to learn, are now able to carry and can learn a lot of good information from all the free videos, podcasts and other quality sources online. The change in carry permit law benefits them.

Since the first edition of this book was published the number of new gun owners has increased significantly. Groups such as the Liberal Gun Club, A Girl and a Gun, and the National African American Gun Association have grown as gun ownership becomes more diverse and urban. These groups do a great job promoting safe and responsible gun ownership, including promotion of instruction. They are likely doing a better job of motivating the untrained than state mandates did.

Gun journalism has changed, particularly in the content of the magazines published by the National Rifle Association and US Concealed Carry Association, the two largest national gun groups. The traditional gun and accessory reviews are still present, but now many pages in those publications offer training and tactics tips from highly qualified trainers. In my observation there are more well-credentialed trainers writing for the remaining print publications (and their online sites) than in the previous decades.

If "Culture Can Change" as we noted in the first edition, the change is coming from these groups and the attitudes of new gun owners, whose primary education in firearms begins with online content. As a result, as the popularity of permitless carry expands, it is the new gun buyers and gun carriers that are bringing the positive culture change with them.

Chapter 8
Instructor Standards

Having established that training beyond the basic is needed, trainers must then address the following question:

How does the gun training industry change the existing narrative to make competent training more accessible to those not currently seeking further instruction?

As more people enter the training business, checking credentials and choosing an instructor become more difficult tasks for the students. As Tom Hogel, KR Training assistant instructor, has stated, "Potential students pick firearms instructors like they choose plumbers: word of mouth, online search results, and name recognition. They can't tell one certification from another beyond 'NRA' and 'law enforcement.'"

Tom has observed that the average gun owner does not understand the difference between NRA Basic Pistol instructor and NRA Personal Protection Outside the Home (PPOTH) instructor, though the two certifications are vastly different. The NRA Basic Pistol instructor certification requires two days of training (and completion of the NRA Basic Pistol course as a student). The PPOTH certification, by itself, requires 30 hours of instruction, not counting the hours spent getting the Basic Pistol and Personal Protection Inside the Home ratings that are prerequisites. In reality, someone with the PPOTH instructor rating probably has 55 to 60 hours of instructor training, which is 3x to 4x the training the NRA Basic Pistol instructor has. Does this matter to the prospective student? In most cases, probably not. The brand value of the NRA instructor rating is high with the general public, even as its brand value decreases within the insider ranks of those who are serious about training higher level courses.

Some private sector instructor ratings are relatively easy to obtain. Others, like the Rangemaster and Paul Howe's Combat Shooting and Tactics (CSAT) instructor certifications, require shooting at USPSA B-class (or higher) level in addition to meeting other standards. The United States Concealed Carry Association (USCCA) has launched its own instructor certification program, which requires shooting at roughly the NRA Basic Pistol instructor level. A few instructor programs have no timed shooting tests as part of their certification process and discourage instructors (and students) from evaluating their skills using timed drills of any kind. They have been successful in raising national "brand awareness" of the program name, but my interactions with and observations of gradates of that type of program has been that their shooting skills are not up to the standards required for the more rigorous instructor classes. People who had ratings up to, and including, NRA Training Counselor and Personal Protection Outside the Home instructor could not pass the beta version of the NRA's Practical Pistol Coach certification course. Multiple graduates of the USCCA and Combat Focus Shooting instructor programs could not pass the shooting standards for the last Rangemaster basic instructor class I hosted. While those experiences cannot be used to infer that all graduates of those programs have deficient shooting skills, they do serve as examples of the relative difficulty of the certifications.

Even someone who accrues all of those instructor ratings may not have a lot of experience teaching actual students until they start offering classes. My standard advice to those seeking to become an excellent instructor was given me by Greg Hamilton of InSights Training Center, early in my development as a shooter and trainer. I don't remember Greg's exact words, but it was basically this:

> Go take the level 1 class at every major shooting school you can. Train with all the most experienced, most credentialed instructors. Learn what they teach and how they teach it. If possible, work as an assistant to them to get more experience before you become a lead instructor. Work on your own skills. Learn how to coach yourself.

I worked toward that goal in two ways: traveling to courses and hosting some of those top trainers locally. After I had taken the course once, I was able to work as a range assistant the next time I hosted the course. That enabled me to see the course from the instructor perspective, and required me to understand their material so that I could coach students and use the same terms to properly support their program during the class. When I teach NRA instructor classes, I invite graduates of those courses to come assist with our basic classes as unpaid interns. This provides them opportunities to get more teaching time in, without the additional work of scheduling and promoting courses or investing in all of the training aids and other support materials needed to run a quality course. Those who have friends and family eager to train with the instructor-in-development are encouraged to invite those people to the class the trainee is working, so they can benefit from our existing infrastructure and program, as well as get the coaching from the trainee they wanted.

The certification process for KR Training assistants includes (1) taking the course as a student and passing it, and then (2) assisting with a session of that class as an unpaid intern, to observe and learn what goes on behind the scenes and what tasks the assistants do during that course. After at least one session as an intern, I (and my senior assistants) give the intern feedback and decide whether they can serve as a paid assistant for future sessions or need more coaching. That process occurs for all the different short courses in my program. Those at the senior assistant level become familiar enough with the material that they can run the firing line or run activities on their own, and a few are certified to serve as lead instructor for some of the courses, earning "lead instructor" money. Anyone trying to develop his or her own training school should strongly consider this type of approach, even if it's simply partnering with other similarly skilled trainers in your area. This process makes the combined program stronger and allows for larger classes without compromising student/teacher ratios. This mentoring/apprenticeship approach was common at the major fixed location training schools (Gunsite, Thunder Ranch, Rogers, Mid-South, and others) in the 1970s and 1980s. It's only been in the last decade or two that the model changed to "lone individual trying to teach 16-24 people by him/her self in a weekend as a traveling trainer."

Just as with selection of plumbers or any other service provider, name recognition, recommendations from others, and online presence matters, typically more than credentials do. Consequently, some lower-tier instructors have become "Grand Masters" at social media and increasing their name recognition, while some top-tier instructors have clunky websites with limited (or no) social media and YouTube video content. Between the two extremes is a wide mix. Those not already interested in training are probably not reading the blogs or following the forums frequented by the insiders and serious shooters. Consequently, a trainer who is trying to reach those who do not currently train may have to become more active in putting content out that likely customers will see.

One manifestation of the lack of careful consideration can be found by watching a process that occurs daily on forums frequented by those at the state-minimum or no-training levels. *The barely trained shooter will ask advice on a topic and orient to the response that is most popular, with little/no concern for screening those answers based on the expertise of those responding.* That lapse often results in accepting recommendations for low-cost products that are widely available from big-box outdoor and discount online retailers, products generally not recommended by mid- to top-tier trainers or by those serious about shooting and defensive handgunning. One thing I am going to start doing (or focus on doing) is reformatting my responses to frequent questions into blog posts that I can simply post links to. That process will make it easier/faster to respond to those questions and include more detail than a few lines. I have also observed that blog posts and YouTube videos are perceived differently from personal responses in forums.

The term *derp* has grown in common use in the gun culture to refer to products and training that have features or characteristics that are considered bad, unsafe, unwise, or dangerous by the serious shooter/professional instructor community. Sadly, it is quite common these days to find instructors spending far more time on producing videos and social media content than on putting in time on the range, taking courses from established trainers, pressure-testing their own skills (in competition and/or force-on-force scenarios), or any other form of professional development. A recent list of the 40 top 'influencers' in the gun industry, based on number of social media followers and subscribers, showed that the majority of them were not instructors nor top-tier competition shooters. In fact, most have limited credentials – and that lack of credentials has clearly had no impact on the appeal or influence of the content they produce on firearms topics. The conclusion here seems to be that not all change is good: social media and marketing skills help build training programs but do not guarantee competent instructors. And social media content from unqualified sources can be, and likely often is, mistaken for professional advice from subject matter experts by average gun owners.

During his instructor development course, Rangemaster Tom Givens commented, "There are not enough competent instructors in the industry to teach everyone who actually needs training." The data support that claim. If 10% of US gun owners decided tomorrow that they all wanted to take 16 to 40 hours of high-quality pistol training from someone at the USPSA B-class level of skill or higher—an instructor who has training in how to teach others to draw from concealment, shoot from cover, and employ other defensive pistol skills—there probably are neither enough people capable of running those classes nor enough facilities to support them. The growth of USPSA and IDPA competition is similarly limited by the size of the pool of facilities and people capable of putting on safe matches and working with new competitors.

A topic that has come up several times in the past few years at the instructors' banquet at the annual Rangemaster Tactical Conference is the need for some sort of "mark of quality" that would aid students in identifying which instructors are recognized by their peers as competent. One model that has been considered is the American Pistolsmiths Guild (APG). To become an APG member, the applicant's work must be evaluated by a certification board. A similar process for instructors would require certification reviewers to attend a course taught by an applicant instructor. Several disconnected groups, each headed by credible national level trainers, are pursuing that goal (as of 2018-2019).

The problem with this system is brand recognition. A decade or two ago, awareness of the APG was higher than it is now, mainly due to frequent mention of it in articles about custom guns in printed gun magazines. Gunsmithing work was mostly 1911 and revolver work that required more attention to detail and machining skills than many AR parts assemblers and polymer frame Dremel users have. That skill gulf has led to a situation in the gunsmithing world identical to what has occurred in the instructing world: quantity of social media content and name recognition matters more than quality of work.

Many (most) of the experienced instructors I know actively avoid derp at every opportunity. They have no wish to see others polling untrained, unskilled people on forums to get questionable or bad advice. They participate only in closed forums frequented by knowledgeable, skilled gun professionals or visit specific sites that are derp-free and promote quality content. However, that avoidance technique results in derps propagating unchallenged and unquestioned in the broader community. In order to change the culture, the narrative must be challenged and improved.

I think the narrative that needs to be promoted avoids getting into derp debates about which holster or which caliber or which gun. If the conventional wisdom is changed from "meet the state minimum" to "training to a real standard"—dry-firing weekly, with at least one live-fire session monthly, and attending at least one class per year, changes in holsters and calibers and guns would occur as a natural consequence of pursuing that higher level of skill. There needs to be an incremental raising of the bar to a level that is higher but still possible for most gun owners.

One challenge facing the training community is that the narrative from trainers conflicts with the narrative from the gun sales and gun politics communities. The message from the sales world is that new gear is the solution to everything, and the items people want most are what get produced and promoted. The message from the gun politics activists is focused on eliminating restrictions of all kinds, including elimination of mandatory training for concealed carry permits. Trainers, by comparison, focus on negative outcomes and want people to carry larger guns and train to higher standards, or risk being killed on the streets. Obviously, what trainers want students to do are harder tasks than carrying the tiny sub-caliber pocket gun in the $20 nylon holster or open carrying freely with no training requirement. The trainers' message is not an easy message to sell for a couple of reasons. First, reports of armed citizens' failing are not common, and second, they are not widely discussed when they do occur because they do not support the most popular narrative.

TOPIC	SALES PERSON	POLITICAL ACTIVIST	TRAINER
SKILL	NEW GUN = SKILL	NO SKILL TESTING	NO SKILL = DEAD
GUN	YOU NEED VARIETY	GUNS FOR ALL	CARRY SAME GUN EVERYDAY
CALIBER	STOPPING POWER!!!	NO CALIBER MINIMUMS	LESS THAN 9mm = DEAD
CAPACITY	FIVE IS ENOUGH	NO LIMITS	LESS THAN 10 = DEAD
HOLSTER	LOW COST, FITS ALL	NO LIMITS	JUNK IN RETAIL STORES
STANDARDS	STATE MINIMUM	2nd AMENDMENT RIGHT	HIGHER STANDARDS
CONCEAL	TINY MICRO GUN	OPEN CARRY	MEDIUM/FULL SIZE

KR Training graphic

Another challenge faced by trainers and those seeking to raise the gun culture bar is the poor quality of the advice frequently given to gun buyers by untrained employees of ranges and retail stores. Retailers and ranges often work on low margins, which keep wages low and limit investment in training and development for staff. Time spent in training is time away from the range or the sales floor, so untrained staff are forced to "wing it." Part of the problem goes back to Dunning-Kruger. No one beyond the total beginner will admit that his or her gun handling is unsafe, whether he or she can define standards for safe gun handling or not. Sales people and range officers do not want to appear uninformed because professionalism drives sales. Consequently, they will attempt to provide answers rather than say, "I don't know." In the absence of professional-level training or serious study, they repeat what they have read or heard as definitive truth. In addition, keeping customers happy requires going along with their existing bad ideas, selling derpy products, or tolerating sloppy gun handling in order to make the sale or risk losing their business to a competitor. Unfortunately, when the sales person or range officer nods his or her head or looks the other way, that tacit approval creates a perception that the idea or behavior is acceptable, making the trainer the bad guy when he or she has to explain not only that the idea or behavior is bad, but also that those who went along with the derp are part of the problem.

Additionally, the need to improve knowledge and skill is not limited to range officers and sales people. In many cases, students who take their first class from me took their state mandatory carry permit class from another instructor, often someone who stopped his or her own training after he or she met state minimum instructor standards. Twenty-three of the 50 rounds fired in the Texas License to Carry (LTC) shooting test are supposed to be fired double action by students who bring traditional double action style guns to the course. The LTC instructor course teaches that students are required to de-cock the pistol each time they return to a ready position. Yet I continue to have students show up for classes who have passed the LTC course but have to be constantly reminded to de-cock. Too many admit that their LTC instructor allowed them to shoot all their shots in single-action mode. I have had a few students show up carrying double action/single action (DA/SA, sometimes called Traditional Double Action, or TDA) guns cocked and unlocked (in the holster, round chambered, hammer back), who did not learn from their LTC instructor that their gun is not safe to carry (or drop-safe) in that mode. LTC instructors and NRA Basic pistol instructors are part of the front line of experts advising the 99% of gun owners who do not train beyond the minimum.

Part of changing the narrative or changing the culture of the gun community must focus on improving the knowledge level of that front line. Within the instructor community, promoting the idea that every instructor needs to attend one class, shoot one match, or participate in other training annually for their own professional development should be the goal. Texas requires its LTC instructors to attend a one day re-certification course every two years, to get updates on any gun laws changed during our legislature's biannual sessions. South Carolina has mandatory annual training for their Concealed Weapon instructors also. As far as I know, those programs are unique among all states that require mandatory training for carry permits.

Chapter 9
Instructor Qualifications

Being qualified as an instructor is more than completing an instructor training school. Here are some different types of certifications, experience and achievements to consider when deciding whether the instructor or a specific course is a good fit for you.

Documented Shooting Proficiency

In section 3 of this book, we will discuss how to evaluate drills and shooting tests, relative to a national measurement scale (US Practical Shooting Association classification rankings). USPSA ratings start at D and advance through C, B, A, Master and Grand Master. Similarly, the International Defensive Pistol Association has rankings that begin at Novice and progress to Marksman, Sharpshooter, Expert, Master and Distinguished Master. These rankings are also used in NRA pistol matches and Police Pistol Combat (PPC) events.

The typical graduate of a police academy is likely to shoot at a USPSA C class level or IDPA Sharpshooter level. Military personnel that are not either military police or in a specialized, higher level unit have probably had much less pistol training than a police officer. SWAT or law enforcement instructor level shooters, and military "operators", have probably reached USPSA B class/IDPA Expert level skill.

NRA or US Concealed Carry Association instructor certifications do not require a particularly high level of shooting skill, and many NRA/USCCA instructors teaching state level carry permit courses may be down in the USPSA D/IDPA Novice level. Neither NRA nor USCCA basic instructor training requires drawing from a holster, so having those certifications does not imply that the trainer is expert in, or qualified to teach, that skill. NRA and USCCA do offer higher level certifications, but even the most difficult of those to attain only require USPSA C/ IDPA Sharpshooter level skill.

The Rangemaster Instructor Program holds its students to a much higher shooting standard. The Rangemaster first level Instructor program requires drawing from concealment and shooting at a USPSA B/IDPA Expert level. The Advanced and Master instructor courses offered by Rangemaster require USPSA A/IDPA Master level shooting to pass. It's unusual for anyone to fail an NRA or USCCA instructor course. Failure rates of as high as 20% are not unusual in the higher level Rangemaster instructor classes.

"Documented", in this context, means that the person performed that skill on demand in front of others, in a class, or at a match. Due to the ease with which videos can be manipulated (best take out of 100 tries, changing frame rate to speed up the action, deceptive camera angles to mask being closer than claimed to the target), it's unwise to use "I saw them do this on YouTube" as equivalent to documented shooting performance.

Actual Incident Experience

If the topic of the course is defensive, not just technical shooting, the instructor's life experience in armed incidents should be relevant. Law enforcement officers are likely to have experience most relevant to the armed citizen, since cops are dealing with the same armed criminals, within (almost) the same deadly force laws as armed citizens. Cops have much more freedom to draw their guns, and also have a duty to act in situations where armed citizens can retreat or flee. Military combat experience is relevant, but military combat usually involves rifles, machine guns and bigger weapons operated by armed teams operating under wartime deadly force rules. Some trainers with military experience do a great job of translating it to be relevant to armed citizens; others are content to run students through military simulation exercises in their classes.

As Claude Werner has taught, **gun battles** occur between teams of armed people, **gunfights** occur when 2 or more people exchange shots, and a **shooting** is an incident where 2 or more people may have guns, but only one (or one side) fires. Many armed citizen defensive situations, and some law enforcement line of duty incidents, are shootings and not gunfights. Similarly, there are those that have experience drawing guns and pointing guns at others (armed citizens and cops), in situations where shooting may have been legal, but was not required. Don't discount instructors that have that type of experience, as the ideal outcome to any incident in which guns are drawn is that the threat of deadly force is sufficient to de-escalate or solve the problem. According to many different surveys on defensive gun uses by citizens, the 'gun displayed but not fired' situation is by far the most common.

An instructor that hasn't been in a gun battle, a gunfight, a shooting or even a defensive gun display may still be able to teach valid and useful information, if that person has been taught by, and/or studied the works of others with extensive experience in actual conflict. That person should be capable of more than simply showing the state- or nationally-certified slides on the topic. An instructor serious about ensuring that they are teaching credible, validated material in this area should seek out opportunities to learn from those with real world experience, including experience with the legal system.

Legal Experience

This category is often linked to real incident experience, particularly for law enforcement officers. Someone that has been involved in an incident where shots are fired and people injured or killed will also have experience giving a statement, being interviewed and going before a grand jury. Some will also have the unpleasant experience of having their case go to trial and depending on a jury to decide their fate. Instructors that are also attorneys with prosecution or defense trial experience bring firsthand knowledge to the classroom that others will lack. Those that have testified in court or worked as expert witnesses on either side of a case also have specialized experience that a basic level instructor does not have.

Below the level of those with firsthand courtroom experience are those that are certified by their state to teach their state laws related to gun carrying, gun ownership and use of force and deadly force. At the top of that tier are law enforcement officers that enforce those laws and have non-shooting courtroom experience, particularly LEO instructors that teach those topics in their local police academies. Instructors at this level should be doing continuing education and professional development to stay current with cases and law changes. Law enforcement officers will receive that instruction as part of their job. Many states do not require carry permit instructors to do any additional retraining when laws changes, and this can lead to some instructors teaching outdated and sometimes wrong information without realizing it. As with the area of instructor shooting skill, the instructor that stops learning and improving when they meet state minimums should be avoided.

Training History

Any high quality instructor should take at least one course a year as professional development. In a perfect world, that course would be from someone outside their normal bubble. For example, a law enforcement instructor with a resume filled with courses taken from other cops and former military personnel should consider taking a class from a pure private sector trainer with either competition or armed-citizen, concealed carry focus, or both. Someone that mainly focuses on pistol skills should take a legal class, or a force on force scenario course, a medical class, or an unarmed skills course. A person that has 1000 hours of training all with a single school or within a single circle of similarly-minded trainers will understand that material very well, but may not understand the content or value of training from 'outside' sources as well as someone with a broader background.

There is an unfortunate tendency in the training world for instructors skilled in one area to take a 2-5 day course from another trainer, and immediately return home to offer their own version of that course. In some cases this is encouraged, as trainers will offer instructor certification courses in their own programs. A few days' instruction in a topic doesn't make someone a true expert in it, however. Courses taught by instructors newly certified in a topic aren't going to be as good as classes taken from the original expert, so consider them as useful introductions but not a replacement for the class your instructor attended.

If you can't find a list of the courses or schools the instructor has attended, and vague terms such as "competition shooter", "law enforcement / military experience" are used, that's an indicator the person doesn't have a strong resume and is hoping no one will ask for details. Those that have done the actual work are typically proud to tell others about it. Number of years in the field, number of hours of training, number of different areas of study, number of trainers/schools, and other statistics mean more than certifications, in my opinion.

Trainers that haven't taken a class from anyone in more than 5 years should be of particular concern, unless the goal is to learn all you can about dated techniques out of historical interest.

Adult Education Knowledge

Shooting instructor classes don't always include instruction in the basics of adult education. Instructors that have training and experience teaching other topics bring classroom and coaching ability to their courses that others may lack. This is particularly true at the state carry permit level, where instructors that read canned PowerPoint slides can make mandatory classroom time painful and pointless.

Skill at coaching physical activities can be extremely valuable, as a skills coach for other sports has developed the ability to observe and correct technique. Being able to perform well is one thing; being able to observe and coach others is a different skill. Some great shooters can do both, but not all – particularly those that started young or progressed quickly in their shooting. Someone with experience coaching those that struggle, due to physical limitations or any other impediment, may have advice to offer that the "natural shooter" may lack.

Years of experience, as an adult educator or even as a shooting instructor, may mean something, or it may not. The person that has had a career teaching state mandatory classes, turning the crank through the classroom and qualification exercise over and over again for a decade, could be great...or terrible. Sometimes 10 years' experience is really one year of experience repeated 10 times. If the instructor's program has not changed, particularly if the material they teach is no longer taught by most others in the field, their course may be of limited value. I've had more than a few students that had to re-learn their shooting grip and stance, for example, as a result of training with older trainers that continue to teach techniques that fell out of favor with the rest of the training world 20+ years ago.

Similar to years of experience, number of students taught can be great...or terrible. Some instructors motivated primarily by profit will attempt to teach large classes alone (example: 24 students on one firing line with one instructor calling drills and no line coaches). This is a profitable way to operate but not necessarily in the best interest of the student. Individual trainers that limit class sizes to 8-12, where they run two relays and only have 4-8 on the line at a time, sacrifice profit for class quality and provide a better value to the student.

The professionalism of the trainer is another area to consider. If you are wanting a 'gun bro' experience, where the instructor drops f-bombs every sentence and frequently tells war stories about their police or military experience, there are trainers who fill that market niche. Some of them are excellent subject matter instructors as well. It may be useful to separate out the fan experience or desire to take a class simply to be around an industry celebrity from the desire to learn relevant skills. Outrageous behavior is great for generating clicks and views and growing social media followers, but it doesn't necessarily enhance the quality of a course. My own bias is to seek out trainers who treat the job of firearms instruction as serious business, staying on topic during classes, speaking in professional terms, and avoid politics or other irrelevant topics that might annoy or offend students. It's all fun and games until the content of what was said or taught during a class becomes evidence in a trial. Flippant comments about "finishing shots", or "have a plan to kill everyone you meet" appeal to a certain audience, but can be problematic when presented to a jury during the trial of a student involved in a questionable shooting incident. Similarly, what instructors (and their students) post on social media is all harmless fun until the prosecution reads it in court.

Student Performance

Ultimately what matters is the benefit to the student. Will you shoot better, will you learn something useful? Some highly skilled technical shooting trainers mainly attract other highly skilled students, who come to classes purely to earn that trainer's pins and awards to improve their own resumes and generate social media content. Those students will then extol the praises of those trainers, despite having done most (all?) of the hard work on their own, outside of class time. You should seek out trainers that have had student successes, in matches, on the street, and in court. Take particular note of students that report that an instructor's training was of value to them in solving a problem or showing them the way to practice moving forward. Often the real value of a class is not what is learned during the course as much as the homework the student does after the course to reinforce what was presented. Online student class reviews can be helpful, and don't be shy about reaching out to those that post reviews with questions about their experiences in that class or at that facility. When you find an instructor you like, find out who they trained with, and consider training with both your newly chosen instructor and their guru when opportunities occur.

Chapter 10
Removing Barriers

Prospective students for shooting training beyond the minimum required by the state are very good at manufacturing and articulating barriers to continuing their shooting education. For the serious shooting skills trainer, the question becomes:

How can a training facility offer a program that helps people overcome the most commonly identified barriers and attract a wider audience? The National Shooting Sports Foundation's market research has identified several reasons why people choose other activities over shooting:

- Other activities offer more exercise.
- Some people want to seek new and different experiences.
- Some other activities are less expensive.
- Other activities may be preferred by family and friends.
- Some other activities may offer more benefits.
- Some other activities may seem more challenging.
- Other activities require less travel for training, practice, and/or competition.
- Other activities may be safer.
- Other activities may have fewer restrictions.

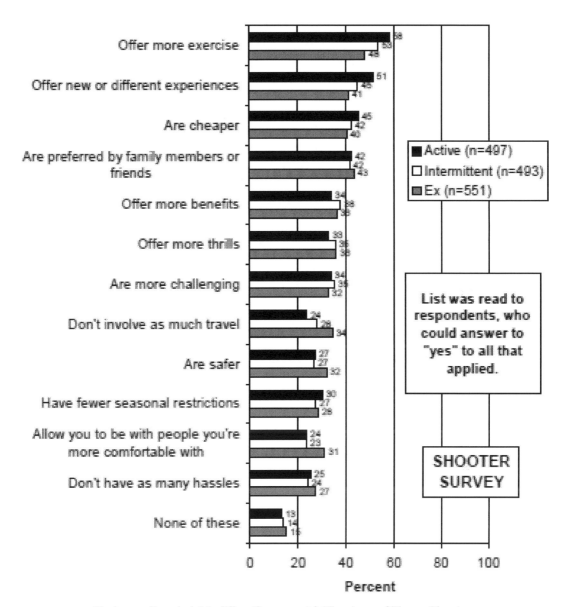

Understanding Activities That Compete with Hunting and Target Shooting,
National Shooting Sports Foundation, 2011

A study of currently active target shooters, infrequent shooters, and those who had recently done little or no shooting produced the following list of reasons for not shooting: time constraints (40%); age/health (30%); cost (18%); lack of access (5%); and other interests/activities (5%). Not surprisingly, time showed up as the #1 reason that people are shooting less. After all, time is the most limited resource most people have. The adjacent chart shows one set of poll data indicating how people spend their time. TV viewing habits are changing with streaming, DVR, Netflix, and other methods of viewing, but it still consumes a lot of time.

Leisure time on an average day

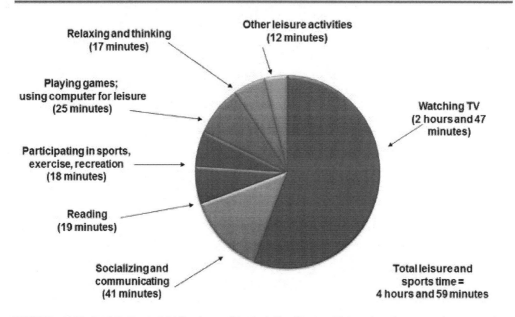

Relaxing and thinking
(17 minutes)

Other leisure activities
(12 minutes)

Playing games;
using computer for leisure
(25 minutes)

Watching TV
(2 hours and 47
minutes)

Participating in sports,
exercise, recreation
(18 minutes)

Reading
(19 minutes)

Socializing and
communicating
(41 minutes)

Total leisure and
sports time =
4 hours and 59 minutes

NOTE: Data include all persons age 15 and over. Data include all days of the week and are annual averages for 2015.

SOURCE: Bureau of Labor Statistics, American Time Use Survey

Much of the current trend in training is for courses to be more physically demanding, particularly those run by younger male trainers coming from recent military service or active law enforcement duty. The acronym OFWG (old fat white guy) has become a derogatory term used by some gun bloggers, but the demographics of NRA membership as well as the Texas License To Carry program, show that older people of all genders, races, and body shapes are gun owners. The good news is that older people often have more time and income because children are grown and because individuals are farther along in their careers or are retired. Often, growing older also increases concern about risk of being attacked (motivation to train) and recognition that more physical options may have lower probability of success than use of a firearm. With age comes reduced endurance and reduced physical capacity, however. While 10-hour days in the hot summer sun or winter cold and drills that require lots of getting up and down may appeal to eager 20- and 30-year-olds, these active trainings may deter 50+, 60+, or older students from attending.

Hours per day that individuals age 55 and over spent doing selected activities

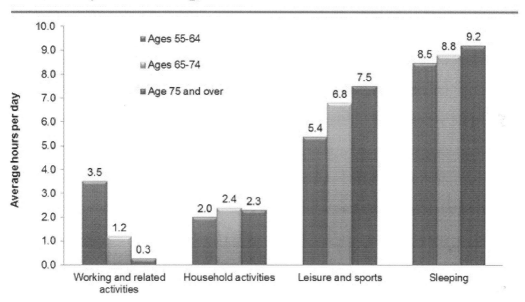

NOTE: Data include all days of the week and are averages for 2011-15.

SOURCE: Bureau of Labor Statistics, American Time Use Survey

NSSF data identifies more reasons why people choose other activities. Ex-target shooters identified lower costs and improved range environment as two key areas that would entice them to return. Unfortunately, to have a range that is clean and well run typically requires not only staff, but high-quality staff, who may cost more than minimum wage cash register operators. And most of the costs are beyond the control of trainers and range operators, who must cover the costs of being in business, with some profit to live on, from tuition and/or range fees. Part of the cost of training is round count, and one way to lower the effective cost to students is to reduce the number of rounds fired in a class. During the ammo shortage that occurred after the Sandy Hook mass shooting event, we adjusted the curriculum of several classes to have less live fire, which made those courses more accessible to students.

Shooters who are inactive list several issues as deterrents to rejoining the sport: extra equipment required, an unwillingness to purchase gear, confusion about what gear to buy, lack of assurance that newly purchased gear will continue to be used, lack of commitment to carrying outside the car, not planning to carry a big gun at all (particularly in a hip holster), and not allowed to draw at the range. Some issues were strong negatives with former target shooters, with competitive shooting being the least popular. Understandably, those who have not participated in an activity in a long time may not want their return to be a test against people who are serious about it. The low numbers for training look bleak; however, 38% of the ex-target shooters viewed access to training as a positive, much like the availability of loaner guns or a family day. Since we are trying to get more than 1% involved, a number like 38% is still a positive.

The need to purchase appropriate gear is one of the reasons people have given me for not coming to the classes I run that go beyond the state minimum. When I became serious about shooting, I had gun club friends who loaned me gear to try and guided me toward better products. At KR Training, we have had so many problems with students coming to our Defensive Pistol Skills 1 course with unsuitable holsters, no mag pouches, insufficient magazines, ill-fitting, low-quality hearing protectors, and other bad gear that we started doing a pre-class gear check for every student as they arrive, to head off problems before we had to deal with them on the range.

Make no mistake, gear is expensive. The gear a shooter needs to attend the typical 2-day defensive pistol course can cost hundreds of dollars, depending upon how rare/costly spare mags for his or her gun are, or how difficult it is to find the exact holster he or she wants. And I do recommend that students going past the state minimum invest in a shooting timer (I prefer the Pocket Pro I for its simple user interface), because having a real timer for dry practice is much better than a phone app. Having gear that makes practice easier also makes practice more enjoyable. If a shooter enjoys his or her practice, he or she will practice more. The other side of the coin is that spending the money on the gear also motivates a shooter to use the gear he or she has spent money on.

Obtaining appropriate gear is particularly challenging for left-handed shooters and ladies, since the majority of what is stocked in big box retail stores and small gun shops consists of the lowest cost products for the most popular guns. Consequently, the majority of retail gun stores do not stock left-handed holsters or dropped- and offset-style holsters. Students who do not have the right gear for class will sometimes rush out the night before to buy what they need, with the mindset that they do not want to spend a lot on gear they are only going to use for one class. Those last-minute purchases often end up being a terrible waste of money, often on gear we do not even let them use on class day because they show up with mag pouches with snap flaps, universal-fit nylon holsters, gimmick holsters, or SERPA holsters. As previously discussed, students who get advice by choosing the most popular response to a question asked to a pool of untrained people also frequently end up with bad gear.

The lack of inclination to purchase appropriate, well-fitting gear is a legitimate deterrent that I have addressed by investing in loaner gear. Over the past 15 years or so, I have built up a collection of more than 50 holsters for the common guns we see used in classes, some purchased personally to test and evaluate, some purchased on close out/clearance deals, some traded to me by students in exchange for credit toward tuition in classes, and some purchased specifically to have as loaner gear. For someone planning on teaching more than a few classes a year, particularly teaching people their first course past the state minimum level, loaner holsters are an excellent long-term investment. Comp-Tac recently came out with their Q-series of holsters that can be set up for right- or left- hand use, with or without dropped and offset belt plates that fit multiple firearm types. Safariland makes a universal mag pouch that fits a huge variety of magazines. Other items we have in our loaner pile at KR Training include spare mags for popular gun models, 10-round mags for single stack 1911s, loaner hats, loaner cover garments, and loaner belts. The clearance section of many online retailers have all yielded deeply discounted items that went into the loaner bin.

Another big loaner item is electronic hearing protection. I bought multiple sets of the Howard Leight Impact models after dealing with too many (often older) shooters who had difficulty understanding range commands on the firing line. Any time I see NRR-19 rated, ill-fitting passive ear protection on top of a head with gray (or no) hair, that person gets offered a loaner set of electronic ears. As someone who is both a frequent shooter and a performing musician, I totally understand (and live with) noise-induced hearing loss, and I appreciate being able to hear better on the range with good-quality electronic muffs.

All of these loaner items benefit my staff and me as much as or more than they benefit the students. All of those items I listed were added to the loaner gear because providing that gear to a student solved a problem that was making it hard for the student to learn the material being taught or because the loaner gear made it safer for the student. I strongly believe that the availability of loaner gear—the ability to come to class and see it, use it, and ask questions about what to buy during class, as opposed to having to commit to buying good gear in advance of class—has been a tremendous benefit to students and has motivated some to attend who might not have otherwise come to class. For a trainer, investments in loaner gear make sense because students may become long-term clients who attend multiple classes over many years. Additionally, those repeat students are likely to generate word-of-mouth referrals that lead to new customers. Investments in gear also make sense to instructors who may want to set up their own online store or stock an inventory of recommended products for resale to students.

Admittedly, some students use the loaner gear and never invest in their own gear, particularly those who take our first 4-hour class and do not return for the higher-level courses. But even in that situation, they gained an understanding of what good gear is, learned how to use it, and came to at least one class beyond the minimum, all of which is a win.

Chapter 11
Strategies

After considering risk assessments, motivations to train, selection criteria for instructors, and barriers to continued training past required minimums, another question to be discussed asks:

What other suggestions might be useful in increasing accessibility and encouraging continued gun training/education beyond the required state minimums?

The previous chapter addressed offering loaner gear to beginning students so that they do not have to incur major costs to take more than the courses required by states to shoot or to carry concealed. KR Training has invested in a variety of guns and extra magazines, belts, holsters, mag pouches, eye and ear protection, and cover garments. As stated previously, gear for more advanced trainings can cost several hundred dollars, an investment that many are unwilling to make without having confidence that they will continue to use the equipment. In reality, the loaner gear benefits both the students and the instructor. Sometimes, students arrive at the classes with guns that are available to them but not right for them to shoot. The guns may be hard to shoot, unreliable, broken, or simply too big for the shooter's hand. Terrible holsters are also a common problem. Some students do not bring enough magazines for the class as it is designed, or they arrive with an inadequate belt or no belt at all. Eye protection is a must, and electronic ear protection is superior so that range instructions can be heard by all participants. Adequate equipment yields fewer problems for both the students and the instructor, and few problems equates to a more positive experience for students and acts as an invitation to return for another good time.

Course length and cost can also affect the willingness of students to acquire training past required minimums. Historically, private sector training started with 3- to 5-day "vacation" classes at fixed locations, like Gunsite, the Chapman Academy, John Shaw's school, and the Rogers school. Classes were often held on weekdays. Those schools and many others are "destination" facilities that offer capabilities and training beyond what is available at many local facilities. Instructors from those schools and graduates of those schools began offering "weekend warriors" 2-day weekend classes, hosted at local and regional ranges. Currently, dozens of instructors all over the country offer hundreds of classes in this format annually, typically 16 to 20 hours of training for $400 to $800.

Most of the traditional NRA classes were 12 to 16 hours, offered locally. As more states began passing concealed carry legislation with required training, the minimum hours for state mandatory training began dropping. For example, in 1996 Texas required 10 to 15 hours of instruction; now, Texas requires 4 to 6 hours. NRA revised their Basic Pistol course to an 8-hour format and developed a Personal Protection In the Home course that covered many topics common to defensive pistol courses (except for drawing from a holster), also in an 8-hour format, in response to the national trend toward shorter training.

Training hours is an area where those serious about training and those passionate about gun politics disagree. The 30- to 40-hour programs originally designed by the fixed location schools were based not on meeting state minimums, but on teaching the skills that instructors felt were actually needed by people training to use handguns in self-defense. Opinions as to the standards of skill performance and the topics to be learned really have not changed much since the late 1970s. The problem, as gun politics activists point out, is that the "best practices" standards of the big schools, if used as state minimums, would restrict the right of self-defense to those with the excess money and time needed to meet those standards. Often, those people are at much lower risk of criminal attack than those with smaller budgets and lower incomes.

More than a decade ago, KR Training converted most of the courses it offers into 3- and 4- hour blocks designed as a series. Teaching everything someone needs to know in a 4-hour class is an impossible task. Consequently, the burden is on the instructor to prioritize skills in their course design. The competition for course time is comprised of family and job responsibilities, other interests, and, of course, dollars. The reality is that more people can spend 4 hours, $100, and 200 rounds on a Saturday training class than there are people who can spend $500, 20 hours, and 1,000 rounds on an all weekend course.

Those who study adult education understand that deeper learning takes place if it is spread out in smaller chunks over a longer period. Students who come to a 4-hour course, pick up some new skills or corrections on old skills, spend the next month working on those specific things, and then return for another 4-hour block tend to progress better and maintain that improvement better than the student who spends his or her entire training budget for the year on a 5-day class at "Disneyland for guns" and then does no practice for months afterward. This lack of follow-through is one reason why so many "level 2" classes in that extended format are disappointingly heavy on review of level 1. Unfortunately, many of the "destination training" customers are the personality type who mistakenly believe that passing level 1 (with no practice to maintain skills) makes them ready for another giant dose of new material a year or more later.

Using a half-day format allows incredible, customer-focused variation in what is offered. For example, if the state permit course is a half-day training, an afternoon follow-on course might focus on teaching more gun skills. Pair a pistol class in the morning with a long gun afternoon course. Pair two classes that are back-to-back in skills progression together to make a full training day. Offer a morning beginner class and an advanced class in the afternoon. Offer a discount to advanced students to assist with the morning class to improve student/teacher ratio for beginners. Perhaps the most important advantage, however, is that more granularity allows better matching of student and course. Anyone who has participated in many classes has had unfortunate experiences: a class where half of it was review; a class where half of it ended up being remedial work taught down to the least prepared student; or a class where at least one student showed up, only to discover the class was way over his or her head. In any of those circumstances, the class ends up being wasted time and money.

Why, then, do so many instructors offer 2-day courses instead of the 4-hour format? Reasons range from "everybody teaches 2-day courses," to "that's not enough time to teach anyone anything," to the ever-popular "I need to make more money than that." Of course, instructors coming from out of town need to make a minimum for the trip to be worthwhile. I have done my share of that kind of road work. But there are far more locally based NRA and state permit-level instructors and local clubs running matches than there are traveling trainers. Thus, the 4-hour format is viable for a majority of instructors who are teaching in their own areas.

After the first edition of this book was published, we began receiving information from other trainers, particularly those offering training beyond their state's carry permit level. One trainer in Ohio, Robert Jewell, reported that more than 5% of the students that took their state permit course at the range where he teaches (whether they trained with him or another staff instructor) returned for a 5 hour "Next Level" course, during the 2016-2019 period. Other trainers have reported increased response when shorter courses were offered to make the transition into higher level training less costly and time consuming.

My advice to traveling trainers is this: design the first part of the program to be accessible to a wider audience and to support a larger class size. Sell that program as a stand-alone short course that is both part of the longer course and a separate item. That format will enable a traveling trainer to reach more students, including some who may take the longer course on a return visit, and will generate revenue that may make a marginally attended longer course fiscally viable. Depending upon the capability of their local course hosts, traveling trainers could design a 4-hour, certified pre-course that the local host could offer as a way to screen and prep students coming to the longer course. This co-training format could minimize problems with students' coming to classes that they are ill prepared and/or ill equipped to attend, by providing a path for them to complete the necessary preparation and/or acquire equipment prior to class day.

Blended learning, where online and in-person trainings are integrated, continues to increase in popularity. At KR Training, I continue to increase my use of blended learning, sending students pre-class articles to read and videos to watch to help them be better prepared for class. This practice is particularly useful when the class is only four hours long and there is little time to deal with remedial students or equipment problems. Emails to students after class and/or monthly newsletters provide drills to practice and articles to read to keep the student interested in (or at least occasionally thinking about) the material they learned in class. The NRA took a big step in that direction in 2016, converting their Basic Pistol course to a blended learning format, over loud objections from a majority of active instructors, who felt left out of the decision process (because they were). The NRA blended-learning Basic Pistol course contained a consistent lecture and professional content in a mandatory format of 6-8 hours online and 3-4 hours of personal instruction. I wrote one of the few public in-depth reviews of the online course, from the perspective of someone who had developed both online, blended, and in-person training in my job at TEEX. The NRA missed the mark, in my opinion, for several reasons. The class was too long and too detailed, including topics irrelevant to the target audience (such as single-action revolver usage and scoring bullseye targets). The result of their offering was poor response from students and angry instructors, who complained to the NRA Board of Directors. The NRA's concept of integrating online and personal instruction was timely; however, their misstep goes back to a general reluctance in the training world to believe that anything can be taught effectively in less than a full training day. Their course became optional in April of 2017.

More recently the state of Texas started approving online training as part of a blended learning approach to meeting state carry permit training requirements. The four hours of classroom lecture required for the permit can now be taken online from a number of certified online schools, and the remaining two hours of the course are to be completed with any LTC instructor. Even though it offers the convenience of being able to complete the training as time is available without traveling to a facility, many people appear to want the interaction that comes from in-person lecture and instruction. Thinking about my own experiences with online training, I believe that another factor is individual discipline. Driving to a facility and getting the training done in a single dedicated block will lead to completion. It's too easy to start an online course and never complete it. Since the first edition of this book was published, the number of KR Training's LTC students choosing to take their classroom training online has dramatically increased, with more than 50% of them now choosing the blended learning option.

My experience has been that if thought is given to prioritization of skills and re-use of technique for multiple tasks (for example, teaching a ready position that is part of the draw stroke and the position where malfunctions are cleared and reloads are performed), it is possible not only to teach a useful subset of skills but also to build a foundation that makes progressing in later classes easier. KR Training offers over a dozen different short courses, grouped together into basic, intermediate, advanced, and instructor-level tiers. These courses include Basic Pistol 1 and 2, Defensive Pistol 1 and 2, tactics courses, scenario-based force-on-force courses, and skill builder/drills classes. I add one to two new courses to the program each year. Response to my 2- to 3-hour Skill Builder class has been strong: it is an "accessible to all levels" course that provides the thing students want most—live fire shooting time, in a format similar to the amount of time they would spend on their own, with value added in the form of structured practice and instruction. In 2017 we announced our Defensive Pistol Skills Program, which combines multiple short courses, some mandatory, with a variety of elective options, that awards a challenge coin to students who complete 40 hours of training, meet state carry permit licensing requirements, and pass the Three Seconds or Less shooting test with a score of 90% or higher. Response to the program has been excellent. Many students who previously might have not have returned for follow on training are now setting their goal as completing the 40-hour sequence, which includes live fire, force on force scenarios, low light shooting, lecture sessions on mindset and legal issues, and analysis and discussion of actual incidents captured on video. Simplification of the different groups of courses into a single program has made it easier for students to see the path of progression.

Like many trainers, I send a monthly electronic newsletter. I limit myself to one email per month to students: I want them to think about KR Training, but I do not want to clog anyone's e-mail to the point that they unsubscribe. I confess to having an aggressive opt-in policy; anyone who emails me about a class is added to the monthly newsletter distribution. People seem to find that tack less annoying than having a "subscribe to my newsletter!!" giant popup in their faces every time they visit the site. I also use targeted emails for specific classes, both to encourage those who have taken class X to take class X+1 and to invite those who took class X in the past to come back as a discounted-price, refresher student.

Breaking the idea that each class is a "one and done" thing and that there is no value in re-taking a class as a refresher student is one of my goals. I see that occurring with Craig Douglas' Extreme Close Quarters Combatives course. I have taken it 3 times, and people commonly talk about the number of times they have taken it. Other than maybe the Rogers pistol course, there is not really any live fire course that people see as a recurring training event. Everyone wants level 2, or the same material from someone different. In reality, there is great value in going back through a class for a second or third time. The returning student will pick up details he or she missed the first time or will simply perform better. As a course host, I have had the opportunity to take or audit many classes multiple times, such as InSights Street and Vehicle Tactics, Rangemaster Combative Pistol 1, Ben Stoeger's 2-day competition pistol course, and the Massad Ayoob Group MAG-20 classroom course.

What do students want? The adjacent chart shows which courses were most popular in KR Training's program over the past 12 years. Demand for the advanced-level pistol classes was the highest, driven by a small number of students who have taken dozens of classes that I have taught or hosted. The least popular (despite my strong belief in their value and continued efforts to schedule and promote them) were force-on-force and unarmed classes.

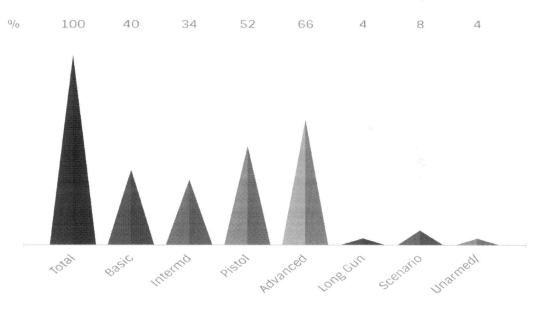

KR Training graphic

Why is generating repeat business difficult? Many people have limited interest. Remember that 99% are only going to do the state minimum and never come to anything else. With that number in mind, the percentages of those returning are not surprising. At KR Training, 25%

who took one course returned for more, 5% took 5 to 9 courses, and 2% took more than 10 courses.

As in any other endeavor, the first step in creating a customer who is going to come to more than one class is to get him/her to one class. The following list focuses on people who might have interest in training beyond the state minimum, or in some cases, training to prepare to meet the state minimum:

Those who want to complete a carry permit course
New gun buyers
Martial arts/MMA students
Those who participate in other shooting sports/activities
Video gamers/paintballers/Airsoft
Seniors
Professionals

To attract new business, USPSA champion, author, podcaster, and trainer Ben Stoeger advises giving away content online. I noticed this concept first in the music business, as a performing and recording artist with multiple CDs of original music for sale in physical and online forms (look my name up on all the standard online places for music downloads and streaming to hear them). Nobody buys music anymore, but they will still pay to attend a live performance. Often, the decision to go see the live show is not based on radio airplay, but on exposure to the performer's content via free online services. In the 1990s, I put a lot of effort into adding content to the KR Training website, but I did not migrate to other platforms (YouTube, blogging) as the trends changed. I did make that migration on the music side, with lots of videos from my own live shows on YouTube, but not as much on the firearms training side.

To initiate an active online presence, start with something interesting to say and then find a way to put it out there frequently enough that people get used to seeing that content. Look at the output critically, because any tiny flaw in anything put out will become the story and the focus of all the internet traffic. Try to make the content as troll-proof as possible. I suggest disabling comments. Nobody reads the comments, and 99% of what is posted in the comments is not worth reading.

Coupons are another useful attraction tool. I ran my first Groupon deal this spring, with decent result, primarily bringing customers who had not trained with us before into classes. Groupon likes to promote particular types of deals: often 50% discounts or 2-for-1 deals, at lower price points. So do not think of Groupon as a primary revenue generator. Its value is in filling seats that otherwise would have been empty and in expanding awareness of the offered program.

Make it clear in your marketing and from your behavior online, that your classes are welcoming to all law-abiding people regardless of age, gender, race, sexual orientation, religion, or political beliefs. The key word is "law-abiding." It is appropriate to require a carry permit for classes who teach skills beyond the state minimum. Being passionate about the right to self-defense and gun rights in general can be done in a professional way without demonizing those who are different from you, particularly those who do not hold your exact political views on a wide range of topics. If the goal is to get more people to attend your classes, the only reason to turn someone away is concern about potentially unsafe or violent behavior.

Understand that your reputation and image are a 24/7/365 effort, not just on class day. Using the f-bomb like a comma in order to sound tougher, or whatever you think it is doing for you, is a bad idea. If you want to be perceived as a professional, act like a professional. Doctors, lawyers, professors, politicians, and public speakers of all kinds do not use profanity and vulgarity as part of their standard communication. Can you use profanity as a deliberate tactic in communication with potential threats? Yes. But understand that in a world where virtually everything you do in public could be recorded and shared with the world by someone. Whether you want it shared or not, language affects perception, perceptions affect juries, and juries may hold the fate of the rest of your life in their hands. Using profanity should be done with the same precision and deliberation you apply to drawing and firing a gun. Unless it is essential, it is more likely to turn off potential students, or students already in your course, than it is to impress them.

The biggest thing I learned from my personal experiences and from my research was a greater awareness of the divide between the noble motives claimed by most who attend training and their actual motivation. The types of training people seek out is rarely what a logical training needs assessment, based on realistic risk assessment, identifies. Training competes with other purely recreational activities for customers' dollars and hours. Those offering training have to seek a balance between the lengths and types of courses customers want, as opposed to what trainers would prefer they attend, in a perfect world. An aspiring instructor must understand his or her customers and students. He or she should keep in mind that shorter and cheaper sells better. He or she should do everything possible to ease new students into the class/sport. As he or she strives to stay in touch and encourage continuing training, he or she must be a coach, not a salesperson. Hopefully, these ideas and thoughts will be useful to anyone wishing to continue his or her own training, as a student and/or an instructor.

SECTION 2: MINIMUM COMPETENCY FOR DEFENSIVE PISTOL

Chapter 12
Why Minimum Competency?

Minimum – the least or smallest amount or quantity possible, attainable, or required.

Competency – the ability to do something successfully or efficiently.

When it comes to the use of a pistol for self-defense, minimum competency would be the least amount of skill and ability needed in order to use that gun for successful self-defense.

What would that be?

Karl and I see people at gun ranges who blaze away at a target three yards in front of them, and they are barely hitting paper. We see people slow plinking, taking one slowly and carefully aimed shot, checking their target, taking their time to set up again for another shot, repeat. We see videos of people attending "tactical band camp" training, throwing lots of lead, but are they hitting anything? Are they doing anything effective? We see people passing their Texas License To Carry shooting test, and their B-27 target looks like it was peppered by a shotgun blast. We see people who are really good at shooting competitions, but struggle with defensive concepts.

Is this enough true skill and knowledge to survive and win? Sometimes in life it doesn't matter if our assessment of our competency is different from the reality. But in a case like this, when your life is what's at stake, you need to be aware of your skill and ability. The Dunning-Kruger concepts discussed earlier in this book apply here. If you don't know what it takes, if you don't know what you can and cannot do, well…what's that going to get you? I started to think about what a minimum set of drills would be to define this concept. That is, **if you shot these drills and could not do them cleanly on-demand, then you don't have the**

minimum competency. Anyone who thinks "I've got what it takes," can make that assessment by shooting the drills and comparing the score to the minimum requirement.

The customer for these minimum standards is the average carry permit holder: someone who carries a pistol on their body, or in a purse, bag or pack that's within reach, for self-defense in a typical incident. It should be a standard that just about anyone can attain and maintain, using their actual carry gear. My process for identifying that minimum is different from what was used by state governments to set carry permit standards. My standards won't be used for licensing. Those who can't meet the standard won't have a fundamental right denied by government. When that issue is injected into the discussion, those opposed to carry permits want the standards as high as possible, to make the permits harder to get, and those in favor of gun rights want no standards (constitutional carry) or the standards set as low as possible. Similarly, government standards often include a mandatory number of training hours. My goal is simply to define a set of performance standards relevant to the specific purpose of carrying a handgun for self-defense: being good enough with it to have a reasonable chance of success if shots must be fired.

This isn't to say once you can do these drills then you are done and can rest here; no, because this is minimum. Trainer, 3-time gunfight survivor and SWAT instructor Paul Ford has observed (based on his experiences and analyzing incidents involving other officers) that in a gunfight you will do about 70% of your WORST day at the range. Think about that. Take your worst day (under the ideal circumstances of the range), and now make it a lot worse, and that's how you'll do. If this is how it goes, how good do you think you really need to be so when the flag flies and your skills degrade to being "worse than your worst," then that level is still high enough to get you through? So, you must train well beyond these minimums. But that said, if you cannot perform to the minimum, the sooner you can know that the better. The sooner you can work to remedy it.

Hasn't this already been defined? Well, maybe. There are dozens and dozens of handgun shooting drills and tests and qualification standards. Every police department, sheriff's office, federal agency, state carry permit program, and training school has at least one. Many have multiple courses for different applications and levels of skills. If we have so many standards, do we really have A standard? Well, we do have to consider these standards are likely within a particular context, i.e. qualifying for police, state carry permits, competition, and other applications. Furthermore, every trainer wants to have their own set of standards and performance assessment. Are their standards truly testing something? Are they well thought out towards achieving a particular end? Or did they just string together some exercises so they could put their name on a shooting test? Is there already a "standard" or "drill" that is trying to answer the question I'm asking?

Note: the details of many of the drills and tests referenced in upcoming sections can be found in the "Drills" section of this book, and all of them can be found online.

Ultimately, my motivation is trying to bring some cold truth to the average carry permit holder. I speak to people all the time who passed the Texas LTC shooting test, including those who shot a perfect score. They are quite proud of their accomplishment, and consider that the end – that they have passed the LTC test, they know all they need to know, that they are as proficient as they need to be, and will be able to handle themselves should they ever need it. I speak with people who grew up around guns, who learned to shoot in the back pasture, but it's evident from watching them they really couldn't shoot their way out of a paper bag much less deal with a response to being assaulted. I'm no expert, but I've learned enough to know that I don't know.

Furthermore, I know it's better to have your bubble burst when it doesn't matter, than to see your world fall apart when everything is on the line. If I'm in the business of helping people protect themselves and their loved ones, I'd like to see what I could do to come up with a simple way to help people assess if they truly have the minimal skills or not.

So then, what is minimum competency? The Texas Legislature and Department of Public Safety think the Texas LTC Shooting Test is minimum. Karl formulated the "Three Seconds or Less Drill" that's based around the typical gunfight, and this test gets used in the various Defensive Pistol program classes at KR Training. But there are many accounts of individuals successfully defending themselves who had no training, or training less than the Texas program requires. Claude Werner has his own statistical analyses of gunfight realities. One could argue it's mostly (only?) important to have a gun and draw it, since the estimated number of annual defensive gun uses (somewhere between 500,000 and 2,500,000, depending upon which set of survey data you use) far outnumbers any estimate of justifiable self-defense shootings each year.

Defining "minimum competency for defensive pistol" is hard. However, just because it's hard doesn't mean we should avoid doing it.

Chapter 13
Framing The Problem

It is not as difficult as playing the violin, but it is a bit harder than riding a bicycle. When it is achieved, adequate pistolcraft produces in its owner a peace of mind unknown to other people – as long as they are armed, awake and aware. – Jeff Cooper, 1996

I think before Karl and I can answer the question, it's important to define and frame the problem. If we're going to define minimum competency for a self-defense situation, then we need to define the characteristics of a self-defense situation. We're not hunting. We're neither military nor police (though it's possible there's some overlap). We're private citizens going about our daily lives, but having to deal with robbery, assault, burglary, rape, etc., and refusing to be a victim of such crimes.

Tom Givens has examined incidents of FBI and DEA agents, along with the 60+ student incidents he's had. What are the common threads?

- Distance between victim and assailant? Up to about a car length, but exceptions can occur (i.e. out to 25 yards)
- You're in plain clothes, gun is concealed, and you need fast access.
- Occur in public areas such as parking lots, shopping malls. Home is rare.
- Shots fired? 3-5, on average
- Multiple assailants are not uncommon

What Tom's data concludes is that a typical private citizen "incident" is:

- armed robbery in some form
- 1-2 assailants highly likely
- 3-7 yards
- limited response time
- "3 shots, 3 steps/yards, 3 seconds"

I know I lean on Givens' teaching and data a good deal, but Tom is a top-notch researcher. Certainly to an extent he's biased, but what Tom is biased towards isn't necessarily "pro-gun, rah rah". Rather he has a bias towards helping people stay alive in the face of a violent world (his training facility was located in Memphis, where the violent crime rate was one of the highest in the United States), and to do so you better have a solid, methodical approach towards finding the truth and what really works; anything else will get people killed. So I consider Tom's research serious and genuine. Besides, you don't have to take his word for it, the data is out there, so you can see for yourself.

Another way to look at it?

It's the ability to get multiple hits, in a small area, from "close" range, quickly.

Unfortunately, if you just say that, everyone's going to define it their own way, so we need to have clear definitions and create standards based upon the clear definition.

In her book *Effective Defense*, Gila Hayes described a simple test:

- 5 shots
- in 5 inches
- at 5 yards
- within 5 seconds

Some people refer to it as the "forty-five" drill, some the "4×5" or "5×4" or "4^5" or "5^4". The NRA uses a 5x4x4 version: 5 shots into each of four 4" circles, with no time limit, in the 2018 version of the NRA Basic Pistol course. Claude Werner has a 5x5 variation, adding "repeat the drill 5 times to eliminate luck and ensure consistency". Greg Ellifritz made a 6×6 variation. However you label it, doesn't that seem to mesh directly with multiple hits? Small area? Close range? Quickly? It's quite a simple drill, and looks like it can fit the bill.

Looks are deceiving though, because most of the variations that drill don't require you to draw from a holster. If the data shows that most incidents are going to be in public spaces, that means you need to be carrying the gun (i.e. it's not on a table, in the nightstand, in the glove box, etc.), which means it's in a holster, which means it's concealed (under clothing, in a bag, etc.). So this implies that you know how to draw and present a gun from concealment. That's actually two implications: drawing from concealment, and being able to carry concealed in public.

If you're going to carry concealed in public, in most American states that means you need to have some sort of concealed handgun/weapons/carry license/permit. Many times that means you have to pass some sort of shooting test. To receive a License To Carry (LTC) in Texas, there is a shooting test. Notice the test is structured around getting multiple hits, (somewhat) quickly, from various "close" ranges. It's a bit better than Gila's test since it works different amounts of shots and different distances, however, it fails on a few counts. First, the B-27 target and "within the 8-ring" is the same size as an 11x17 sheet of paper. That's not "in a small area". Second, just like Gila's, there is no drawing from a holster. Did you catch that? The Texas test for obtaining a license to carry a handgun – which implies a need to draw the handgun out of concealment – doesn't require you to show you can draw the gun from concealment. Note, I'm not advocating changing the test because there are reasons why it is the way it is, but do these tests truly provide you with the needed skills or a false sense of security?

Karl notes: Most state carry permit qualification courses do not require drawing from a holster as part of the course. Many commercial shooting ranges do not allow customers to draw from holsters because so few have had formal training in correct holster use. The most common self-inflicted gunshot wounds occur when re-holstering or drawing, particularly when drawing quickly or re-holstering without looking. Many states use the NRA Basic Pistol course as their state's handgun qualification course. Instructors certified to teach that class are not certified to teach holster use.

Teaching holster use requires the student to have a holster that's safe to use for training. Decades of experience teaching first-time holster users led me to invest in dozens of (more than 60 at last count) loaner holsters because I got tired of dealing with students showing up with low quality holsters purchased at retail stores that had a variety of problems: awkward positions, poor gun fit, prone to coming off the belt due to weak belt attachments, hybrid holsters and soft holsters that closed up preventing the user from re-holstering without muzzling his/her fingers prying it open, gimmick holsters that had to re-assembled to re-holster the gun, and the nylon "fits all" gun bucket. One huge challenge facing the new gun carrier is the reality that most retail stores, particularly the chain stores, do not stock decent holsters because the vast majority of customers do not understand what they need or why the features trainers consider essential matter. Additionally, with dozens of gun models on the market, it's impossible for any store to stock enough variations in holster material, design, and gun fit to have a good choice for every person. As a result, most good quality holsters are purchased online, with no way to "try before you buy." I've found that having the loaner holsters available ensures that students have decent gear to use for class, and they learn what a good holster is and how it works and why you need one before spending money.

KR Training is one of very few schools anywhere that has taken this approach to solving the holster problem. The rest just try to deal with whatever students bring to class, which often increases the number of safety concerns and makes learning the draw stroke harder for the novice. The "just deal with it" approach requires the instructor to have an even higher level of skill at teaching, to work around the challenges that bad gear creates. The problems gets even more difficult when female students are involved, as most holsters designed for male bodies often ride too high and angle in too much for ladies. To simulate the discomfort most ladies experience trying to use a holster designed for men, cinch your belt 2-3" above your belt loops, even with your belly button and try to draw. The only instructor level course I've taken in the past 30 years that addressed that issue was the Cornered Cat instructor class taught by

Kathy Jackson – a class that has been offered very few times and is no longer available now that Kathy has retired from teaching. Women competition shooters proved to be the best source for that knowledge over time, and now some ladies shooting groups, such as A Girl and A Gun, do an excellent job of educating their facilitators and chapter leaders about this topic. Still, many male instructors don't understand this issue at all, particularly those coming from a law enforcement or military background, where "use what you are issued" is the general policy.

Most instructor training programs that certify people to teach others to draw are 2-3 day courses that require a prior basic instructor certification, or 4-5 day courses. Among those who teach that skill or teach others how to teach that skill, the generally accepted process is to teach an open carry draw first, and then integrate the additional complexity of clearing a concealment garment. Many law enforcement instructor and military instructor programs only teach duty-related skills, such as drawing from a retention holster, and do not include instruction in techniques specific to drawing from concealment – so even those who have completed 40 hour or longer law enforcement firearms trainer programs may not truly be "certified in" teaching concealment draw skills.

Due to the higher training hours and higher shooting standards required, and the lack of availability of that certification course, only a fraction of those certified as NRA Basic Pistol instructors go on to obtain the Personal Protection Inside the Home and (holster-certifying) Personal Protection Outside the Home certifications. As a result, the national pool of trainers who have formal training in the teaching of drawing from concealment is significantly smaller than the pool of everyone certified at any level of pistol instruction. A growing number of trainers with no true certification in teaching that skill are teaching it, using their law enforcement or military instructor status (or in some cases simply their law enforcement or military status), or experience as a graduate of courses and/or competitor or certified range officer in matches where concealment drawing is required as justification that they are "qualified" to teach it, because there is market demand.

Yet another challenge to the concept of teaching the concealment draw in the typical state carry permit course is this: a lot of gun owners do not show up for class with the level of disciplined gun handling skills required to begin learning holster use. The untrained gun owner who "shoots good enough" can be found using a cup and saucer grip or thumb-behind-the-slide-just-barely-low-enough-to-avoid-having-the-thumb-sliced-open grip, having to swap the gun from one hand to another or shift their grip to operate the magazine release and slide release, having sympathetic movement of thumb and forefinger when operating a de-cocking lever or other control on the firearm (often combined with inattention to trigger finger position, so this occurs with finger on trigger, sometimes resulting in negligent discharge), a tendency to use the "my gun is heavy" (gun pointed at their feet) or the TV inspired gun-pointed-at-ceiling-or-over-the-backstop "ready" position with little attention to muzzle direction and the consequences of where a negligently fired round might go. People show up for state carry permit classes with guns they've never fired, guns they borrowed from friends, and (my personal favorite) DA/SA style guns that they've never de-cocked, have never shot double action, lacking the hand strength to pull the DA trigger. The average "gun owner, no formal training" needs 4-8 hours of formal training to clean up their gun handling, and attention to muzzle direction and finger discipline before adding the risk and complexity of drawing from a holster is taught.

All of this leads to the explanation as to why drawing from concealment is not taught or required by most state carry permit programs. A limited number of instructors are truly qualified to teach it, there's low availability of training to train instructors to teach it, state mandatory training hours are insufficient to include that topic and cover the required material in the allotted time, many ranges don't allow it, many carry permit applicants lack the disciplined gun handling skills and shooting fundamentals (such as grip and gun manipulation) to be ready to learn the skill, the risks of self-inflicted gunshot wounds increase, and the challenges of students failing to have appropriate gear combine to make including that instruction in a basic "concealed carry" class taught by a large pool of instructors to average gun owners with no prior formal training essentially impossible.

Back to John's discussion about minimum standards...

I will say this.

Both of these tests are something I could label "sub-minimal". That is, they are reasonable tests, but not quite to the standard we're trying to define.

I believe the primary reason for Gila's test isn't so much a proficiency test as a shopping test. That is, if you get a gun, you need to be able to do her test with that gun. If you cannot, that is probably not a suitable gun for you. All too often I see a woman who comes to class with the gun her husband or boyfriend gave her: she has small, weak hands, and he gave her a Sig P226 which she simply cannot operate – she would easily fail Gila's test. As soon as we swap her with a more reasonably fitting gun, her skills and abilities didn't change, but now she could pass Gila's test. In discussing the 6×6 variation, Greg Ellifritz struggled with the Ruger LCP because it's too small of a gun (fit) for him. So perhaps consider this test more of a good way to validate appropriate equipment than skill.

But certainly, if you cannot perform Gila's test (or I'd say Claude's variation, to ensure you didn't get lucky on the one run) or if you cannot clean the Texas LTC, and you cannot do these consistently and on-demand, then certainly you do NOT have the minimum competency. These aren't enough due to shortcomings in the drills themselves, but they are a rung on the ladder. So if these are "sub-minimal" what might be minimal?

It seems we have expanded our criteria:

- multiple hits
- in a small area
- from close range
- quickly
- drawing from concealment

To see what else might be necessary, we can also look at video. Hooray for video! Hooray for dash cams, security cameras, everyone having a phone with a camera, and then a willingness to share all of this on video websites like YouTube. You can see a lot of what really goes on.

One thing that happens often? Hands. Shooting with two hands. Shooting with one hand. There's no question you should try to shoot with both hands. Why? You're faster. This goes back to "quickly", and shooting slower is the opposite of "quickly." That said, the reality of life is your situation may require you to shoot one-handed — and perhaps with your weak hand. You may have something in your hands that you cannot drop, like a child. Or another reality is, sometimes you just start shooting with one hand. I've seen it, I've done it — we know better, but yet something happens in the head and you just start shooting one-handed. It's good to know how to do it.

At this point, a drill like KR Training's "Three Seconds Or Less" drill (discussed in depth in section 3) starts to come into play. This drill was intentionally designed around the "3 shots, 3 yards, 3 seconds" typical gunfight. It works on multiple hits, in a small area, from close range, quickly, drawing from concealment, two- and one-handed shooting.

The drill also adds in another aspect: movement. Do we need to move in a self-defense situation? You betcha. Is it better to shoot, or not get shot? Of course, the answer is "not get shot." Some like to phrase it that incoming bullets have the right of way. Thankfully since bullets only travel in a straight line, a simple but large enough side-step is important. It "gets you off the 'X'", as it forces the assailant to reset their Observe/Orient/Decide/Act (OODA) loop, and well... movement is going to happen.

That's the thing. Movement is going to happen, or at least, it should. Generally, something happens and people scatter, running away from the source of trouble. This of course is a good thing (distance yourself from the problem). However, it's really either move or shoot, not shoot on the move. Paul Howe pretty much says to do one or the other:

> *...shooting on the move, it's a skill all shooters aspire to learn and spend a great deal of time and effort trying to master. I've never had to use it in combat. When moving at a careful hurry, I stopped, planted and made my shots. When the bullets were flying, I was sprinting from cover to cover, moving too fast to shoot. I didn't find an in-between. If I slowed down enough to*

make a solid hit when under fire, I was an easy target, so I elected not to.

As for shooting and closing on a target, it only makes the bad guys accuracy better and walking into a muzzle may help you to test your new vest sooner than you wanted to. Diagonal movement works, but again if you have to slow down too much, you're an easy target, and are generally in the open. Speed can act as your security in this case to get you to a point of cover.

Training to "shoot on the move" with a Groucho Marx walk? Well, nice skill, but is it really important within our context? Howe's case was military, and if he doesn't need it there, would we really need it in the "3 seconds" of a private citizen self-defense incident? A little movement, like a quick and decisive (and far enough) side-step on the draw is good. Much more than that? Not really needed.

So now we're starting to find things we don't need.

Are there other things we don't need, in terms of minimum competency?

I asked Tom Givens, of his 60+ students who were involved in self-defense incidents, did any need to reload? Further clarifying, if so, did any reload as a part of the fight? Or was it administrative after the fight was over?

Tom's response to this question:

None of ours had to reload and continue shooting. I can think of four off the top of my head that went to slide lock, however, further shooting was not required at that point.

Think about reloads. If typical private citizen gunfights are 3-5 shots, that's not even enough to warrant reloading a snub revolver. Of course, that's average. With Tom's students, I think the range was 1 to 11 shots fired, but again, no reloads (though apparently some came close). John Correia, who produces and narrates the Active Self Protection YouTube channel, claims to have viewed videos from more than 15,000 armed incidents, mostly individual defense or law enforcement situations. He estimates than in less than 10 of those 15,000 incidents, reloads occurred during the fight or had any impact on the outcome.

So do we NEED reloading as a minimal skill? It would seem not.

For that matter, how about malfunction clearing, be it a simple failure to eject, stovepipe, double-feed, whatever type. Do malfunctions occur enough that we need to consider them a minimal skill? Again, data would point towards no. This isn't to say it's not useful and good to know, but remember we're looking at minimal competency.
So if you start to look at higher level, longer tests like the FBI Qualification or Rangemaster Level 5, are these reasonable "minimal" tests? Nope. I would say there are somewhere above the minimum. They cover shots out to 25 yards, which doesn't fit the bill of a typical gunfight. They cover reloads. They cover malfunctions. They also cover things like changing positions (e.g. going to kneeling). Again, all good skills to have, but beyond minimum.

Look at any list of well known, widely used tests. At this point, what new skills or techniques are being added? Shooting from kneeling, from prone, around barriers, turn and shoot, multiple targets, transition to a backup gun, disability (e.g. loss of one hand so must do everything with the "other" hand, including reloads), using a light (weapon-mounted or held in the other hand), and the list goes on. Are these skills that are involved in the typical gunfight? Well, maybe one here or there but the exception does not prove the rule. All in all, these sorts of things just aren't being done in the typical incident. Thus, it's hard to argue they are part of "minimum competency".

So have I been able to define "minimum competency" required for defensive handgun use? Not yet. It seems when we look at what unfolds in a typical incident and what needs to be done to handle that typical incident, you get:

- drawing from concealment
- And perhaps moving on that draw
  (like a side-step then stop; not shoot-and-move)

- getting multiple hits
- in a small area
- 5" circle? 6" circle? 8" circle? consider human anatomy
- from close range
- Within a car length, so say 0–5 yards
- quickly
- 3 seconds or less
- using both hands, or maybe one hand (or the other)

In his email to me, Tom Givens said of this:

My list of prime skills for concealed carry might be:
Primary:
presentation from concealed carry
shoot with 2 hands
shoot with 1 hand, both dominant and non-dominant

Secondary:
reload, slide forward and empty gun
fix simple malfunctions like failure to eject, Tap-Rack-Bang

Everything beyond that is certainly good to know,
but unlikely to be used by typical CCW.

All in all, the same set of minimal skills are being presented.

So what you need is the ability to do the above – at a bare minimum. If you cannot do the above, you've got work to do. If you cannot do the above, there is no shame in that, if you use it as motivation to get better. However, there is shame in letting your ego continue to lie to you.

Remember that I am working to establish a minimum.

Let me restate the problem: private citizens being the unfortunate victim of a violent crime. The choice to use a handgun as a tool to contend with their immediate victimization. To use the tool with some measure of effectiveness, one needs some modicum of skill with that tool. And, that you should have a realistic assessment of your skill with that tool, instead of a false impression.

We have to look at what really happens in a violent crime. No, nothing will be perfect, nothing will be absolute, but we can see enough of a pattern if we look at enough crimes, we can then formulate a solution for dealing with it. This is like solving any problem.

That you can plink tin cans in the back pasture is not a standard. That you can pass the Texas LTC test is not an acceptable minimum. You need to be able to draw the handgun from concealment and get multiple fast, accurate hits on a small target within a reasonable distance. You need to be able to do this with both hands, and one hand (each hand). This is the bare minimum. Later in this book we'll provide our top 10 drills, in order of complexity, each testing a wider range of skills. Any of those drills can be used for testing and assessment.

Note: That doesn't necessarily mean to shoot these drills as your practice. Rather, shoot the drills and see how you do (test, assess). See what you do well, see what you need to work on. When you identify what you need to work on, your practice time (both live fire and dry fire) should work on the fundamentals necessary to help that. Formulate a plan and a program to help you achieve the goal of cleaning the drill. Work on those skills for a while, then come back and shoot the drill again. Keep notes on your progress.

Keep in mind the Paul Ford concept of "70% of your worst day." Look at how you're performing "at your worst" and think about how much worse that will really be. Use that as a guide to establish where you really need your skills to be.

So many things push to a higher standard, and that's good. The problem with always pushing for higher standards, to have the most uber-tacticool or difficult challenging drill/test/standard is it starts to make you wonder where the baseline is. Everyone's out to push things high, so how does that look to someone just starting out? Does it make it seem like an unachievable goal? That if it's going to take me 5 years of dedicated work to get there, how does that help me deal with the death threats I'm currently receiving from my crazy ex-spouse? Or if some standards are setting the bar too low, are people getting a false sense of accomplishment and ability that could wind up doing them more harm than good should they need to call on those skills?

You don't need to be a national champion competition shooter or a military "operator" in order to protect yourself. But you likely need to be better than you think you are.

The point I'm trying to make is to not make this the standard to train to, but rather I'm out to bust false senses of ability. I think it's wise to know what minimum competency is, and to not consider "minimum" to mean either some really low-level that's essentially equated to "skill-less" or to mean once you've met the minimum that's satisfactory and you can stop your journey. It's none of those things. It's merely a way to come to some sort of realistic terms of where your skills and ability lie. When your life is at stake, you need honest assessment. Ego or pretense could get you killed. But sometimes it's neither of those; it's simply that you don't know what you don't know, so here's an opportunity to learn.

Chapter 14
Improving the Texas LTC Shooting Test

That said, Karl and I've maintained that minimum competency is not good enough. You need to work to a higher standard (that Paul Ford comment about 70% of your worst day). I would say the current "3 Seconds or Less" drill is a good "higher standard" to work towards. Other good "higher standards" would include the FBI Qualification, F.A.S.T., Gunsite Standards, Rangemaster Level V, Hackathorn Standards, and the 3M Drill.

But again, this is higher. We're talking minimal.

A Possible Minimal Drill?

As much as I hate to say it, I think the Texas LTC test COULD be it. But it needs work.

Here's the drill, shot on a B-27 target, with the 8, 9 and 10 rings counted as 5 points, the 7 ring counted as 4 points and the 6 ring (including the head) counted as 3 points.

3 yards
1 shot, 2 seconds, 5x
2 shots, 3 seconds, 5x
5 shots, 10 seconds, 1x

7 yards
5 shots, 10 seconds, 1x
2 shots, 4 seconds, 1x
3 shots, 6 seconds, 1x
1 shot, 3 seconds, 5x
5 shots, 15 seconds, 1x

15 yards
2 shots, 6 seconds, 1x
3 shots, 9 seconds, 1x
5 shots, 15 seconds, 1x

Here's how it could be changed to make it a better test of minimum competency:

Needs to be shot from concealment.

Current test has you working off a bench, and shooting from a ready position. Unrealistic.

Must shoot from concealment, whatever your chosen carry and concealment method is. If that's from a hip holster under your shirt, fine. Pocket carry, fine. If that's from a purse, fine.

Use a better target.

The B-27 is like hitting a barn wall. Furthermore, it's not anatomically correct.

Use a target like an IPSC or IDPA target. There are a host of such targets out there. The key is a target that provides a smaller "acceptable hit" zone, and that is anatomically correct.

Make scoring more difficult.

It's "hit or miss," "acceptable or unacceptable". There is no graduated scoring scale, it either is or is not. If it's on a line, if it's questionable, score it unacceptable. 90% minimum score, or better, 100%.

Do not adjust the listed par times.

Having to shoot from concealment adds enough time to make the published par times more difficult.

This could be debated, and probably debated per-string. Like the first string (3 yards, 1 shot, 2 seconds) is probably sufficient, but the last 3 yard string (5 shots, 10 seconds), should that time be lowered? Probably, but this is splitting hairs at this point. Keep it simple and keep the test as written. These other modifications are more important.

The 15 yard strings are debatable.

That's a pretty long car, but it does simulate a home defense situation where the shooter in a safe room may need to shoot into a living room or down a hallway. If I was using my above example of needing to get a friend some quick skills in an afternoon, I'd focus on the 3 yards, then on the 7 yards, and I'd skip the 15 yards.

The Modified LTC Shooting Test

We have developed a variation of the LTC test. This modified drill will use the IDPA target, which retains the characteristics of the original CHL target, with smaller (and more anatomically correct) scoring zones. Scoring will also be done with IDPA "points down" (-1 and -3), so simple addition/subtraction is all that's needed to score it. Misses and late shots are -5. The drill is a total of 25 rounds (half of the original LTC 50 rounds). To score it, just count points down. 25 (down zero) is maximum score. 18 (70%) is passing, 20 is 80%, 23 is 90% which would be considered "instructor level". These are the same percentages used in the Texas License to Carry course. The modified B-27 target used for the official state test and the IDPA target are shown side by side, roughly to scale, in the picture below. The B-27 is 24" x 45". The IDPA target is 18" x 30" with a much smaller 5 point zone.

Each string is shot from concealment (or from ready, as noted below). When the gun is at the ready position or holstered, it must be in one of these conditions, with a round chambered:

Single action only firearms (1911 style pistols and similar designs) will start cocked and locked. Hammer cocked, safety engaged.
Traditional double action (DA/SA style) or DA only guns will start decocked

Striker fired guns will start with a round chambered
Use of any manual safeties is optional for DA/SA, DAO and striker fired guns

If someone who was uncomfortable with the idea of carrying a round chambered wanted to run the test, including the task of racking the slide each time the pistol is drawn in their drawstroke, they could. Anyone choosing that approach would be required to start every string that begins with the gun holstered with an empty chamber. From an administrative standpoint this complicates and slows the pace of the test. However, those insistent on this practice, who intend to carry in this mode, will benefit from this exercise in suffering, as it will illustrate how much speed and accuracy is lost as a result. Each string of the test replicates the first shot(s) fired in a defensive incident, thus the need to practice using the mode in which the gun will be carried.

3 yards

The original test was:
From ready, two handed, one shot in 2 seconds (5x)
From ready, two handed, two shots in 3 seconds (5x)
From ready, two handed, five shots in 10 seconds (1x)

The modified test is:
From ready, ONE handed, one shot in 2 seconds (2x)
Gun holstered, dominant hand on gun, support hand on chest, TWO handed, one shot in the HEAD in 2 seconds (2x)
Hands at sides. On signal step left, draw and fire 2 shots in 3 seconds
Hands at sides. On signal, step right, draw and fire 2 shots in 3 seconds
Hands at sides. On signal, draw and shoot 2 head shots

7 yards

Original test:
From ready, five shots in 10 seconds
From ready, one shot in 3 seconds (5x)
From ready, two shots in 4 seconds
From ready, three shots in 6 seconds
From ready, five shots in 15 seconds

Modified test:
Hands at sides. On signal, draw and fire 2 shots in 4 seconds
Hands at sides. On signal, draw and fire 3 shots in 6 seconds
Hands at sides. On signal, draw and fire 5 shots in 10 seconds

15 yards

Original test:
From ready, two shots in 6 seconds
From ready, three shots in 9 seconds
From ready, five shots in 15 seconds

Modified test:
Hands at sides. On signal, draw and fire 2 shots standing, 3 shots kneeling in 15 seconds

The modified LTC test is more difficult than the original Texas LTC test, but not as difficult as the KR Training "Three Seconds or Less" Test, which we use as the standard in our Defensive Pistol Skills program. My changes incorporate some elements of the "Three Seconds or Less" Test for the 3 yard strings and some elements of the current FBI qualification for the 7 and 15 yard strings.

The drill can always be made more difficult by shortening the time limits or using a smaller target for those wanting a bigger challenge. This course of fire that's short and challenging enough it could be run multiple times during a 100-round practice that included drawing from concealment, or broken into individual strings and practiced to develop specific skills. Those running the drill at ranges that don't allow drawing should cut a full second off every string time (except for the strong hand only that starts from the ready position).

Remember: the intent of trying to establish "minimum competency" is because we, as humans, tend to overestimate our skills and abilities. We tend to think we have the skills, and that we'll handle ourselves just fine when the flag flies. It's better to test yourself against standards such as these to see if you really do or do not. It's better to have a dose of reality now, when you can afford it and can then work to remedy any shortcomings.

Chapter 15
How To Get There

So you've shot some tests and determined you need some work. Or maybe you have not and you are not sure where to start and how to get there? How to find where you need to improve?

Karl and I felt like maybe there should be a program to help you out. Like in weight lifting, a program like Jim Wendler's 5/3/1 program is a great way to get going and address a number of topics on the road to building strength. Could such a program be devised for shooting? I think so. Mike Seeklander has developed a program that's covered in his books and DVDs. His approach may work for you.

I think in most regards it's going to come down to the individual. What is your learning style like? Are you self-motivated? Do you have enough to be able to self-diagnose and improve? In the beginning, we all need good teachers, and there are good schools and instructors out there. Take advantage of those opportunities to have a teacher, a mentor. There's a lot of product coming out that can be a help for sure, but I've found that those tend to be most useful to folks that already have a clue. You don't have a be a master, but a rank beginner is going to get a lot more from having a real instructor looking over their shoulder, that can see precisely what's going on and offer ways to correct, improve, and progress.

In terms of mechanical shooting skills, at its most basic level it breaks down to speed and accuracy. Thus, we can manipulate those two variables to help us find where we need improvement and where to focus our efforts. If you are the self-motivated type, pick a drill, a number of which are provided in this book. If you're not sure where to start, go with our list of 10 and start at number one. Shoot the drill as written. If it provides no challenge, move to the next drill, and so on until you fail to consistently clean the drill on demand. When it gets to that point, I like to recommend taking the drill and shooting it without time-limits: focus on the marksmanship aspect of the drill. If you cannot shoot the drill, or a portion of the drill, with no time limits or pressure, you have identified where you need work (perhaps 15+ yard distances). Once you can shoot the drill cleanly without time limits, now put a stopwatch on your shooting: see how long it takes you to shoot the drill as-is. This will give you a par time and starting point. From there, make small reductions in the time. Maybe you start at 8 seconds, so move to 7.5 seconds, then 7 seconds, and so on until things break down. Then you will have identified another place to work. Taking video of yourself can help identify performance issues, as well as having an instructor who can watch you and provide feedback.

You have to practice the things you don't want to practice. You have to be willing to push yourself outside your comfort zone. Another useful element is having a tangible goal. You can have a lofty goal, then break it up into smaller milestones. Perhaps it starts with shooting the Modified Texas LTC clean with no time limits, then you work towards the time-limits. Then you pick a harder standard, like the 3M Drill, with a 15 second par, then 14 second. It may be shooting a drill as-written with a 80% score, then 85%, then 90%, then 100% on-demand every time. As you work, you'll find where your weaknesses are and use dry fire practice to improve those. Be willing to be patient, but work consistently.

In the end, the desire is improvement. That we understand what "minimum acceptable" is so we can ensure we're at least that, but then work to exceed it. Set a new level, then rise above it. And so on, and so on, always seeking to improve.

Chapter 16
Defining A Path To Progress

In 2014, Karl was asked by the leaders of the A Girl and A Gun Women's Shooting League to give a presentation for their chapter facilitators on the topic of skills progression and development. A summary of that material is presented here.

Purchase a shooting timer.

Without a shooting timer, you can't fully measure performance.

Note that there are some cheaper options too, in the form of "shot timer" apps for smartphones (both iPhone and Android). Your mileage may vary with them however, just due to limitations of the hardware microphone being able to pick things up. IMHO, it's not an unreasonable way to start, but long-term you're going to want to pick up a dedicated and proper shot timer.

100% on the Texas LTC test shot using an IDPA or IPSC target, not a B-27.

IDPA/IPSC has a smaller A-zone. Shooting 100% on Texas LTC is basically 25% of GM.

Note: when Karl gives "percent of GM" he's referring to IPSC/USPSA Grandmaster level. This isn't to say you need to shoot at that level, but it gives you some idea of where things lie along the continuum. How to figure out the relative difficulty of any par-timed shooting drill will be discussed in a later section of this book.

Learn to draw from an open carry holster and be consistent in your shot to shot timing.

The classic drill for this is Bill Wilson's "Bill Drill". Draw and fire 6 shots, at 7 yards. The score only counts if all 6 hit the A-zone of a USPSA target or the "down zero" ring of the IDPA target.

Bill Drill = par time of 5 seconds at 7 yards with all A's on IPSC or IDPA target. That's a 40% goal.

Learn to do a speed reload.

Practice the "Four Aces" drill with a par time of 7 seconds, which is 37%. The Four Aces drill is simple: On a USPSA or IDPA target at 7 yards, draw, fire 2 rounds, reload, and fire 2 more rounds. The par time is set assuming that you have a round in the chamber during your reload (a.k.a. the speed reload).

Learn a slide lock reload.

Practice the F.A.S.T. drill. Set a par time of 12 seconds, from open carry. This is a 40% goal. The difference between a speed reload and a slide lock reload is that the gun will lock back and the magazine will be empty when you eject it, then replace it with a new magazine with ammunition in it. This adds the task of closing the slide after the new magazine is inserted. This can be done by grabbing the slide, pulling it fully to the rear and releasing it, as you are bringing the gun back on target (a.k.a. the power stroke method), or you can press the slide lock lever down as you regrip the pistol and bring it back to target. Using the slide lock lever is slightly faster and allows the grip to be re-established sooner, but depending upon the gun model, lever size, hand dexterity, hand size, and how much resistance the lever offers when you manipulate it, it may be very easy to use, or very awkward, slow, and difficult. Not sure what technique is best for you? Run the drill 10 times using the power stroke, and (using your shooting timer), extract your reload time by looking at the time between the last shot fired before the reload and the first shot fired after the reload (a.k.a. your reload time). Write down the fastest time, slowest time, and the average of all 10. Then repeat the drill using the slide lever technique and record the same data.

Then apply Paul Ford's law: assume that under stress your reload will be 70% of the worst run. Choose the technique that gives you the fastest "worst run... If they are close in time, look at the individual runs and choose the one in which you are the most consistent.

Learn how to draw from concealment, and practice shooting one handed.

Shoot a perfect score (20 out of 20) on "Three Seconds or Less". That's a 50% goal.

Learn how to clear malfunctions.

Practice the 3M Drill (discussed in the Drills section of the book). Set a par time of 15 seconds, which is around 50%.

Shoot a complex drill that tests many skills.

For example, shoot the original 90 round IDPA Classifier with a goal of shooting at least 160 seconds (162 is 40%, 130 seconds is 50%).

We'll revisit this idea in the section of the book that defines a longer sequence of 10 drills.

Chapter 17
Minimum Competency –
Revisited Again

In 2014, Claude Werner wrote an article on "Practice priorities for the Armed Citizen." Claude's article gave me a few more things to think about, and perhaps revise/refine in my suggestions for practice and skills progression.

Claude speaks about a progression, a "where do I go from here?" concept. Claude offers his own suggestions, such as using the NRA Defensive Pistol Qualification from the Winchester Marksmanship Program. But what really got me was pointing out a key problem most people have when it comes to live fire practice:

Most people have to limit their live fire practice to indoor ranges where drawing from the holster is not allowed. This presents an issue to those who carry pistol in holsters. I've gotten quite spoiled at KR Training and with good ranges around Austin where you can practice drawing from a holster. Of course, there are still those people who go to one of the local indoor ranges that have restrictions on drawing from a holster, and of course others around the country tend to have these restrictions as well. I overlooked that reality. Claude offers:

> Like many of my colleagues, for a long time I said the hard part of the drawstroke is establishing grip. I've changed my opinion on that. The hard part of the drawstroke is getting the pistol indexed on the target enough to get a good hit with the first shot. John Shaw, a world champion shooter, clued me in to this many years ago. Note that I didn't say a 'perfect' hit.
>
> Indexing the pistol to the target (presentation) is easily practiced from a high ready position starting at the pectoral muscle of the body's dominant side. Starting this way is not generally a problem at an indoor range. And since I recommend

practicing one shot per presentation, the 'no rapid fire'
limitation at many indoor ranges isn't an issue either.

This is one of those "smack your head because you wish you could have had a V-8" moments. What Claude writes is so true. The press-out, the presentation, whatever you want to call it, it's the hardest part and such a vital skill. When you draw? You then must press out. After a reload? You must press out. Clear a malfunction? You must press out. The press out is such a vital skill (it's a key thing stressed in so many of the KR Training courses). And yes, you can practice this at the indoor ranges. You can start from that high, compressed ready position (step 3 of the 4-step drawstroke), and press out and break one shot. While you might end up eventually moving fast in doing this, your single-shots will still be "slow" relative to each other (i.e. you're not double-tapping) and thus no range rules broken. So, so, so true, and so important.

Thank you, Claude, for my "V-8 moment." Regardless, if you take a progression like Claude recommends or I recommend, the underlying issue remains the same: you'll use some particular course of fire to assess your skills, then focus on improving the areas you identified as weak. For example, in one live-fire practice session I shot numerous drills not so much to shoot the drills (i.e. throw lead in a semi-organized manner), but to exercise the fundamental skills I consider important and identify what I was doing well and what I needed work on. I saw I needed to move faster, and doing a lot of one-shot draws are in my future. So yes, working that press-out is in my future.

Another thing Claude touched on.

...to get a good hit with the first shot....
Note that I didn't say a 'perfect' hit.

What I like about it most is that it is a 100 percent standard, not 70 or 80 percent like a qualification course. We need to accustom ourselves to the concept that if we shoot at a criminal, ALL the rounds we fire must hit the target. That's being responsible. These remind me of my concept of "(un)acceptable hit," which I will expand upon shortly. I prefer that phrasing over "good hit" or "miss," because like Claude said, it's not necessarily a "perfect" hit. It's also understanding that all the rounds must hit what we need it to hit; we must make acceptable hits.

Chapter 18
It's Not a Miss, It's an Unacceptable Hit

You're at the gun range practicing. After shooting, you look at your target and examine your holes. Inevitably there are some holes in places you didn't want them. If you are like most people, you call them "misses", note them, maybe a little disappointed, but you chalk them up and move on. The gravity of those holes isn't great.

No longer call them misses.

Call them "unacceptable hits".

Every bullet you fire goes somewhere – *it always hits something*. The question is, is the something you hit acceptable or unacceptable?

If you don't hit exactly what you intended to hit, it does you no good.

If you're shooting for a tight group and get a flier? You blew your group. Unacceptable.

If you're shooting for score and hit outside the top-point ring? You're down points, you lose the competition. Unacceptable.

If you're hunting, nail the deer in the vitals and the buck drops DRT (Dead Right There)? Acceptable. If you gut-shot him and he runs off, never to be found and suffers a slow painful death? Unacceptable.

If someone is attacking you, you must place every bullet in a vital area. This is the only way to (eventually) guarantee the attacker will stop. These are the only acceptable hits. If a shot lands in the stomach or shoulder or thigh? Maybe eventually the attacker will stop, but in the meantime they continue their attack. You failed to stop the attack and the attacker is able to carry on with their destruction; unacceptable.

If in that attack you totally miss the attacker and the bullet lands and damages someone's property? Unacceptable. If the bullet hits an innocent person? Unacceptable. If the bullet hits your spouse or child? Unacceptable.

Every bullet that flies will hit something. What is acceptable is a very narrow band. What is unacceptable is quite wide. The implication is in practice, you must work (hard) to get acceptable hits and nothing else. If that means you must slow down, slow down. If that means you need to improve your sight picture, improve it. If you need more training, get more training. Don't let your practice sessions be nothing but ballistic masturbation – have purpose.

Yes, from time to time we'll still make unacceptable hits, especially if we're working to improve a weak area. But this is about mindset. Recall a story of some competition shooter (forgot who) who became as good as he was because of how his Dad trained him. They would go out to the range and practice. As soon as the shooter made a non-A-zone hit? They packed up and went home. If he wanted to shoot, he had to get only A-zone hits. That's motivation to get only acceptable hits.

You will fight like you train. Train to make only acceptable hits, so when you are in the fight for your life, you'll only make acceptable hits.

Chapter 19
Addressing Assumptions in Minimum Competency

While working on revisions to the KR Training curriculum, we became aware of some assumptions we had made.

Our original work was primarily focused around the gun and shooting portion of the equation. While that was a reasonable focus, if you look a little deeper into the conclusion you can see there are precursors/prerequisites that are assumed or taken for granted. This would be things like basic gun manipulations: how to load a gun, how to unload a gun, how to load and unload a magazine, basic range etiquette, how to practice effectively, how to seek out good training and instruction.

One admirable attribute about Claude Werner is how he often focuses and finds ways to work with people in less-than-ideal circumstances. For example, many gun ranges do not allow people to draw from a holster, or it may be impossible to use a shot timer due to noise levels. Claude often works and formulates curriculum and drills to work within these constraints.

In a recent discussion on minimum competency, Claude presented a drill with a loose structure like:

- Load 7 rounds into the magazine
- Load the gun
- Shoot 6
- Unload the gun

While at first glance it seems odd to enumerate the steps of loading the magazine, loading the gun, and unloading the gun – and some may desire to gloss over those steps – they're actually quite an important part of the drill. They are giving the student practice at loading and unloading, and they give the instructor a chance to observe the student performing these operations to ensure they are doing it correctly and safely.

When discussing a topic like "minimum competency," it's important we mind our assumptions so we do not overlook the complete set of skills necessary for competency.

Chapter 20
Development of the Min Comp Assessment

It's about building confidence through competence.

Introduction

I, John, published my original writing on the topic of Minimum Competency for Defensive Pistol on my blog.hsoi.com on July 11, 2013. In March 2019, we expanded upon the original work in *Strategies and Standards for Defensive Handgun Training.* Since then, my thoughts have evolved and refined. At the 2022 Rangemaster Tactical Conference (TacCon22) I gave a talk on Minimum Competency, presenting the originating work along with my recent thinking, including my attempt to quantify a notion of minimum competency via an Assessment.

I wanted to capture my thinking in creating this Assessment: why I chose what I chose, what I left out, what I left in. Why did I create this? What was my thought process? In doing so it not only explains the Assessment, but I hope it will foster further discussion on the topic of minimum competency. I don't have the answers, but seeking them is a worthwhile endeavor.

Origination

When I say "minimum competency", what I mean is:

When it comes to the use of a pistol for self-defense, minimum competency would be the least amount of skill and ability needed in order to use that gun to successfully defend yourself.

Why is this important? Because people need to have realistic awareness and knowledge of their capability. Do you really know what you think you know? Can you do what you think you can do? Do you know that? No really...do you *KNOW* that? There are many places in life where our illusions (delusions?) can differ from reality with little consequence – this is not one of those places.

It's fantastic when my fellow Texans tell me they obtained their License To Carry (LTC); it's a milestone worth celebrating! To me it is just that: a milestone in the journey. Too many people look at obtaining their LTC as the end, the destination – I have arrived, I am done! I disagree. Yes, you have made it this far, and there is still some road ahead. For example, the "C" in LTC is "Carry", which implies "concealed, in a holster". But where is drawing from a concealed holster in the TX LTC shooting test? It isn't. I'm not saying to change the test (another topic, another day). I am saying within this context, LTC is a milestone, not a destination.

If it's not a destination, what is? Yes, it's good to "be better today than yesterday", but there's merit in knowing what is "good enough". Not everyone is a hobbyist, an enthusiast that wishes to achieve the highest levels of skill. Some people are just "stay safe", "get home to my loved ones each night", "please leave me alone" sorts of people. In fact, given Karl's research into "the 1%", I'd assert the "get home, leave me alone" types are the majority of Gun Culture 2.0 people. Additionally, for each of us our resources are finite: time, money, energy, capacity, gumption, motivation, desire. We must spend them wisely. There is merit in being "good enough" and being satisfied in that so you can pursue other things. If you want to be "the best" that's great! Please pursue that with gusto! If you wish to be "good enough", you ought to know what "good enough" actually means. Remember, there are no promises, no guarantees, but I figure if we can nail down a reasonable notion of "good enough" then well...that's good enough.

Or another way to look at it? What level of skill do you really need to win? Do you really need to be a Grandmaster (GM) level of skill? Or might it actually be sufficient to just have a gun and the wherewithal to use it?

Let me be clear. This is a floor, not a ceiling. The floor can be high. Minimum is not a synonym for low. As well, consider it a "ground floor", as you can certainly build and rise above it.

After examining a few contextually-relevant data sets (Givens, FBI, DEA) as it pertains to private citizen concealed carry for personal defense, a typical incident profile is generated: armed robbery of some form, 1-2 assailants likely, 3–7 yards, limited response time, "3 shots, 3 yards, 3 seconds". If we break down the mechanical pistol skills relevant to such a profile, we can determine what skills may be minimally relevant towards management of a typical incident:

- Draw from concealment
- Multiple (acceptable) hits
- In a small area
- From close range
- Quickly
- Using both hands

Originally, I wanted to determine a good drill that would manifest this notion of minimum competency. That is, if I gave you this drill to shoot now, cold, on demand, you could do it. If you could, that would raise *confidence* in the assessment of your *competence* to perform the skills. I looked at numerous existing drills, such as 5x5 (and Claude's 5^5 variation), TX LTC, Three Seconds or Less, and others. While not ideal, I can assess skill and competency well enough using existing drills. It has enabled exploration, discovery, and learning.

I also consider defining minimum competency important because it guides how we approach teaching. One way I frame this context is: imagine you have a friend who comes to you saying they have credible threats on their life, but they've never thought about a gun until now. "Hey you know about guns. Can you teach me?" What can you do with them in an afternoon? What SHOULD you do with them in an afternoon? Defining minimum competency can help us prioritize and improve the efficacy of training.

Chapter 21
Are You Sufficiently Self-Confident?

What is Confidence?

The feeling or belief that one can rely on someone or something; firm trust. A feeling of self-assurance arising from one's appreciation of one's own abilities or qualities.

Confidence is something we all want to have, especially in areas important to us. When we are confident, we have the ability to perform under pressure – instead of crumbling. It doesn't mean we won't be nervous or scared, but it does mean we know we can and will perform. There are numerous ways to achieve (a higher level of) confidence. One is to ensure a solid grasp upon and ability to apply fundamentals – the necessary base or core.

Michael Jordan, arguably the best basketball player of all time, said: "You can practice shooting eight hours a day, but if your technique is wrong, then all you become is very good at shooting the wrong way. Get the fundamentals down and the level of everything you do will rise."

There are really no super-secret ninja tricks. The best out there are just the best at applying the fundamentals – and they are supremely confident in their ability to do so.

Note this requires not only having the skill, but *knowing* you have the skill *and* knowing that you can apply those skills, on demand, under pressure.

When it comes to defensive pistol skills and concealed carry, there is without question a need – a requirement – to have confidence in one's abilities. You carry because you acknowledge the possibility you may have to defend your life or the life of someone else, so this is a realm where you must have a strong self-confidence. Anything else could put your life – or the life of someone else – at risk.

Step back and think about it for a moment.

You probably think you can handle these things just fine. And maybe you can.

But do you know this for certain?

In the next section, Karl and I discuss our favorite drills and how to assess the relative difficulty of any par timed drill. We think those drills make a good baseline set of drills handgun shooters can use to maintain and develop skills.

Can you shoot and pass these drills?

Let's go back to the original discussion of "minimum competency". I concluded:

> *Have I been able to define "minimum competency" required for defensive handgun use? Not yet. It seems when we look at what unfolds in a typical incident and what needs to be done to handle that typical incident, you get:*

- drawing from concealment
  - And perhaps moving on that draw
    (like a side-step then stop; not shoot-and-move)
- getting multiple hits
  - in a small area
  - 5" circle? 6" circle? 8" circle?
  - consider human anatomy
- from close range
  - Within a car length, so say 0-5 yards
- quickly
  - 3 seconds or less
- using both hands, or maybe one hand (or the other)

That's what you need to be able to do – at a minimum.

Let's just look at the "Bill Drill" because it's a short and simple drill that basically covers the above 6 points. If I walked up to you and asked you to shoot a Bill Drill, right now, in front of me, could you do it? How does the thought of that make you feel? Does it make you uncomfortable? Do you feel butterflies in your stomach? Do you know for a solid fact you could shoot that cold, on-demand, and rock it — or are you not certain?

If the thought of this makes you feel even one iota of uncertainty, then you do not have the confidence you need. If you feel confident, then shoot it. Can you shoot it to an acceptable level? And can you do it again? Or maybe you don't feel anything, and you just admit you don't know. Then well, you need to know.

If you don't have the confidence you need to work to gain it. If you don't have the knowledge, then you need to shoot it and gain that knowledge. This is not a time for believing you're "good enough" with no factual basis to back it up — do not let your ego get you killed; this is not a space where you can "fake it 'til you make it". Your life, and the lives of those you love are on the line. You need a true, honest assessment and knowledge of your skills and abilities — and the confidence that knowledge brings. And once you've acquired that knowledge, now you have measured and quantified knowledge of your performance, which not only gives you an articulable and tangible expression of your ability, but also the confidence in knowing your level of performance.

Have that confidence. For when the flag flies is not the time to wonder if you can — you must already know you can.

SECTION 3: DRILLS

Chapter 22
Developing the "Three Seconds or Less" Test and Target

The Three Seconds or Less test was created with these design goals:

Test the skills most relevant to pistol use by armed citizens.

Those skills were discussed in the previous section.

Take less than 25 rounds to complete.

The majority of our half day courses include 200-250 rounds of live fire. The number of rounds allocated for testing needed to be low, particularly if the test was to be run more than one time during a course. Many of our students only have 2-3 magazines for their carry gun, and for lower capacity guns, 25 rounds may require all 3 magazines. Having a higher round count would likely require students to refill magazines with loose rounds to complete the test, increasing the time required to run the entire drill.

Use only one target.

Not only because a one-target-per-firing-position format is common, but also because it simplified scoring and logistics.

Scoring is simple counting of total hits in a single zone.

Qualification courses with an excessive number of hits, and/or scoring zones with variable point values, are more complex and time consuming to score.

Uses a minimum number of shooting distances.

Moving the firing line to a new distance from the target, or changing the target distance at an indoor range, takes time. Using different target zones (head/body) to simulate the change in target size posed by varying distances can test to the same objective.

Includes the fewest possible par time changes.

Most traditional qualification courses of fire use different par times for each string. The task to be performed is selected first, then a par time set by the test creator, typically with no regard for the par time used for the preceding or following drill. Reducing the number of par time changes simplifies administration of the test.

Uses a target with multiple scoring zones.

The difficulty of the test can be scaled by choosing which scoring zone represents an "acceptable hit".

Uses a target that has anatomically correct scoring zones.

This insures that the test is relevant to armed self-defense.

Uses a target that could be printed on a standard paper size.

This allowed easy duplication

Sets a performance standard that is roughly 50% of USPSA GM

Difficulty level equivalent to most LEO academy standards

Previously, our team had designed a target we called the KRT-1. It included 6 colored shapes, each with a number from 1–3 inside each shape. There are other similar targets available, but they were all created on 24" paper. When used on the 18" wide target stands we have (made mainly for USPSA/IDPA type targets), many of the shapes would be directly over the sticks, which was a problem. So we created our own. It had three colors, three shapes, and a choice of 3 numbers. One of our standard uses of this target is to call a single color, a single shape or a single number. For each of those 9 possibilities, two colored, numbered shapes on the target are designated.

It had 3 rows, with the shapes on each row different sizes, providing varying difficulty (a feature most color/shape command targets lacked). Another way we use this target is to run a drill using both hands on the gun on row 1 (smallest shape), strong hand only on row 2 (middle size), and support hand only on row 3 (largest size).

The target also included two triangular shapes marked A and B, intended to be roughly the same size and shape of the heart/lung area of the chest and the nose & ocular area of the face. Two 1" grid cross hairs were placed in the upper corners for use in zeroing guns and measuring group sizes.

If you use the number on each shape as the number of rounds to fire, you get a command matrix that looks like this:

Command	Shape 1	Shape 2	Total Rounds
RED	Red 1 Circle Row 1	Red 3 Diamond Row 3	4
YELLOW	Yellow 3 Circle Row 1	Yellow 2 Square Row 2	5
BLUE	Blue 1 Diamond Row 2	Blue 2 Square Row 3	3
SQUARE	Yellow 2 Square Row 2	Blue 2 Square Row 3	4
DIAMOND	Blue 1 Diamond Row 2	Red 3 Diamond Row 3	4
CIRCLE	Red 1 Circle Row 1	Yellow 3 Circle Row 1	4
ONE	Red 1 Circle Row 1	Blue 1 Diamond Row 2	2
TWO	Yellow 2 Square Row 2	Blue 2 Square Row 3	4
THREE	Yellow 3 Circle Row 1	Red 3 Diamond Row 3	6

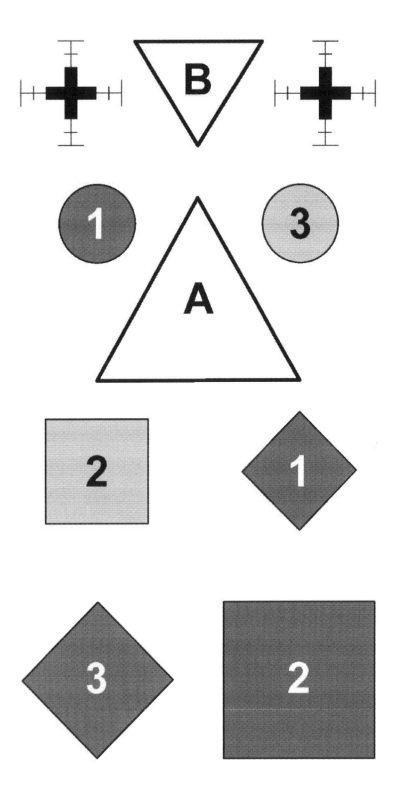

Originally the idea was to use the triangular regions of the KRT-1 for the Three Seconds or Less test, but it was eventually rejected for these reasons:

Only had one scoring zone. The only way to scale up or down the difficulty level would be to change the distances used for the test. Triangular shapes, particularly the chest shape, really didn't match human anatomy as well as a trapezoidal shape.

Inspired by an excellent block of training on the history of target design during the Rangemaster Advanced Instructor course taught by Tom Givens, we looked at a variety of widely used targets to get ideas.

The final version had all these features:

B&W target, printable on 11x17 paper. That means it's cheap to reproduce, particularly for students that want to practice the drill.

The head box is a 6" circle with a ½" black ring. If the interior is used for scoring, this 5.5" circle is roughly the right size to use for the 5x5 drill. The 6" circular shape is the same height and width as the head part of a standard USPSA or IDPA target, and the head of the FBI QIT 99 target.

The white trapezoidal box in the center of the head is roughly the same size as the 3"x5" card used in the F.A.S.T., also similar in size and shape to the upper A-Zone of the USPSA target, also similar in size and shape of the upside down triangular shapes used on many anatomical targets. The inner box of the FBI QIT-99 is 3" x 3".

The black "tombstone" shape used for the outer ring of the chest area is 10.5" x 10". It's slightly smaller than the 12"x13" chest region of the FBI QIT-99, smaller than the 11"x17" C zone on a USPSA target (and the -1 zone on the IDPA target), smaller than the 12" outer circular ring of the NRA-D1. The limitations of keeping the target printable on 11x17 paper bounded the size of that feature.

The gray trapezoid in the chest is 6" at the top, 8" at the bottom and 7" tall. This makes it close in size to the 8" circle used in the F.A.S.T. and the IDPA target, smaller in size than the 6"x11" USPSA target A-Zone. More importantly, it matches the size and shape of the heart/lung area of a standard body quite well.

The center white trapezoid in the chest is 3" at the top, 4" at the bottom, and 5" tall. This makes it close in size to the 3"x5" card used by Dave Spaulding in his 2x2 drill, and a scaled shape similar to the 4" x 6.5" rectangle in the center of the FBI QIT-99. Each of those shapes are similar in size and shape to the human heart.

At the core of the target is a 3" circle. The current industry standard for a duty sized handgun is mechanical accuracy of 3" at 25 yards. This feature was included mainly as a measurement tool for accuracy testing.

There are two 2" dots included in the white space above the shoulders of the primary target. These were added because they could be used for a variety of dot drills, and the limited space remaining on the target made it difficult to add anything larger.

The gray sections of the target are intended to be the primary scoring zones used for testing, with the white zones used as highlighted aiming points, and as the primary scoring zones for a more challenging version of the test. The black outer zone is normally considered a "miss", but can be used as an acceptable scoring zone if a less challenging version of the test is needed.

The neck section of the target is gray with a black outline, with no white insert. Many targets such as the USPSA, IDPA and FBI-Q target do not model the neck very well (or at all). This feature was included to make our target more anatomically accurate.

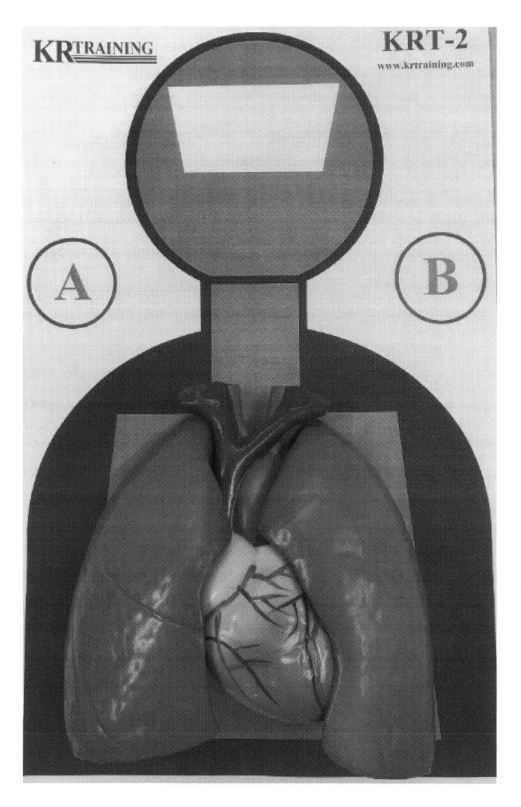

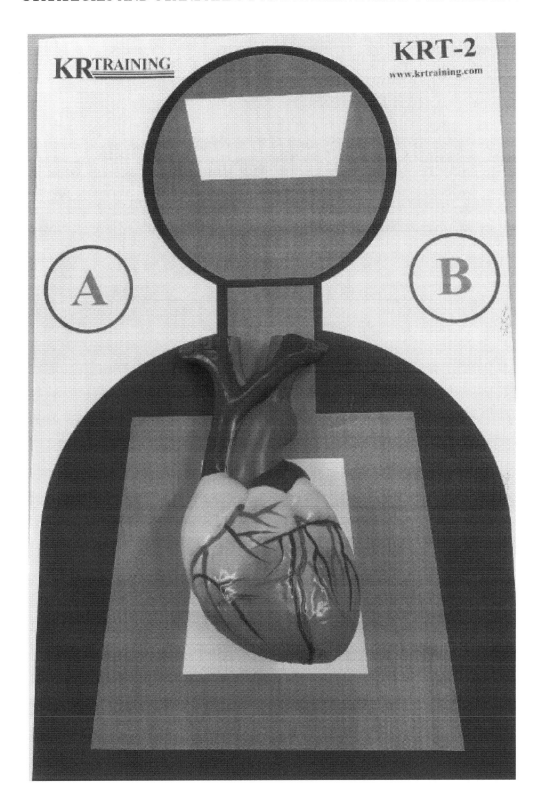

Karl Rehn & John Daub

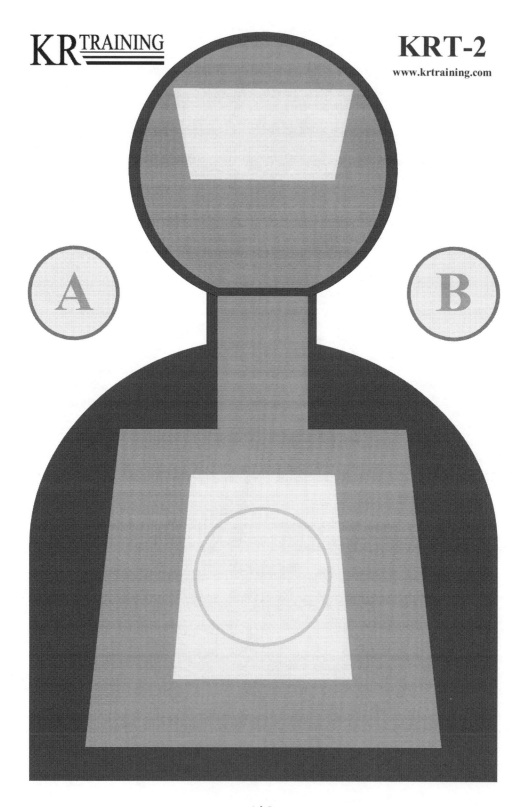

The next step was to design the way the target would be used. 25 rounds was an appealing number, using half of a 50 round box of ammunition. But shooters taking our classes with small guns with 6-8 round capacities would need 4 magazines to finish the test without stopping to refill magazines. We set the round count goal as 20. An early version of the test used 5/4/3 point scoring, with a maximum of 100 points, but for logistic and philosophical reasons, we modified the test to consider hits acceptable or unacceptable, with scoring a simple count of hits inside the acceptable hit zone.

The "3 seconds" concept came from the often repeated line that the typical gunfight is 3 shots, fired at 3 yards, in seconds. So the very first drill of the test would be: take a step, draw from concealment and fire 3 rounds from the 3 yard line, in 3 seconds. Maintaining the goal of using a single par time for each string of the test, all other strings would use that same par time, making the design question "how much work can someone at the 50% of GM level do, on a particular skill, in 3 seconds?" In my study of the last 100 years of handgun training and testing, I am unaware of any handgun test being designed in this way. Is that because it's a bad idea, or just because no one else was ever lazy enough to want to avoid changing par times on a shooting timer a dozen times during a qualification course of fire?

To test multiple skills would require multiple strings. Someone at the 50% of GM level should have a concealment draw of 1.5-2.0 seconds starting with hands at sides. Many qualification courses of fire are designed to be run at the end of 16, 24, 32 or 40 hours of training. This test will be given at the end of 4, 8, and 12 hours of training, the first time at the end of a short course where the student is learning to draw for the first time. Students in those classes often show up with holsters that are sub-par in a wide variety of ways: awkward angles, difficult to reach positions, tight fit, weak connection to the belt, riding so low to the belt that a full firing grip can't be established with the gun holstered, often concealed with a garment that may have its own problems: a tight fitting t-shirt, a dress shirt buttoned all the way closed, or a light weight shirt worn unbuttoned, that's blowing around on a blustery day on an outdoor range. Drawing a loaded gun quickly, perhaps attempting to go faster than the individual's comfort zone, is a high risk activity.

We addressed the risks and problems in several ways, including purchase of dozens of loaner holsters, belts and guns, to provide students loaner gear when the equipment they bring to class is unsuitable. We studied the differences in time to first shot when students used a variety of start positions: hands at sides (open carry), hands at sides (concealed carry), hand on gun/support hand on chest (a.k.a. position 1 of a typical 4 count draw), ready position (low or muzzle level with target). Gun to target from ready is low risk, consistent for most shooters. Concealment draw starting hands at sides is the most complex skill with the most opportunities for errors to occur. Using a variety of start positions (and making the simplest version of the test work from open carry, instead of concealed carry), provides more shooting time per 3 second string and creates a more balanced test of skills.

Starting with the 3 yards, 3 seconds, 3 shots baseline, what other skills need to be practiced at 3 yards? Head shots? One handed shooting? Shooting while moving or retreating? Shooting from a retention position? How much shooting at 3 yards vs. other distances? Over several iterations of the test and reviewing all the data we could find on actual incidents, we decided that half the test should be from the 3 yard line, with two iterations of the step-draw-shoot 3 drill (6 rounds). Those drills required a full drawstroke of around 2 seconds, with shot #1 fired at the 2.0 mark, shot #2 fired at the 2.5 second mark, and shot #3 fired at the 3.00. So split times of 0.4 to 0.5 were required. Hitting the 6-8"x7" trapezoid at that distance doesn't require a perfect sight picture. A target focus and a rough sight picture, with the front sight and rear sight both in view but perhaps not perfectly aligned, is all that's needed.

The other four rounds (of the ten to be shot from the 3 yard line) tested two other types of shooting. The head shot drill, putting two rounds into the 3"x4" box, required a better sight picture, and more time on the sights and trigger press. To provide that time, that string starts with firing hand on gun, support hand on chest. The final string at 3 yards is actually started at 2 yards, and consists of firing 2 shots, strong hand only, while backing up. This simulates a very close range engagement, such as might happen between two parked cars or in a hallway. Those rounds are typically fired from some kind of retention or point shooting (no sight picture) position.

With 10 rounds left of the 20 available for testing, decisions about what distances to use and what skills to test had to be answered. With only 3 seconds available, a drill such as draw, shoot one, slide lock reload, shoot one would likely take too much time for a shooter at the 50% of GM level. Modern data on armed citizen incidents indicates that reload speed is not a critical skill, but there are situations where an armed citizen might have to clear a malfunction or load a gun that had been stored with an empty chamber. Our testing indicated that allowing the shooter to start with an empty gun at slide lock, magazine ready to insert, and requiring them to insert the magazine, rack the slide and fire one round to the body at 7 yards was a skill that most (but not all) could complete in 3 seconds.

Shooting head shots at 7 yards was included to simulate hitting body shots at 15 yards. A string that required a turning draw was incorporated. The final two strings tested strong hand only and support hand only shooting. The necessity of testing support hand only shooting is a topic still debated within our team, as examples of support hand only shooting in actual incidents are extremely rare. As the test has evolved we've simplified that string to allow a start position with gun aimed at the target, with the total rounds fired reduced from 3 down to 2, to minimize the impact of that skill on total score.

Students training in our program shoot the test at the end of each four hour course, with increasing scores required to pass and graduate to the next class in the sequence. The very first class in the sequence is called Defensive Pistol Skills Essentials. It is a marksmanship and gun handling course working only from the ready position, focusing on the skills necessary to pass the Texas License To Carry shooting test at the 90% level. The state only requires 70% to get the carry permit, but we require students who want to progress to the rest of the classes in the sequence to shoot 90% or better on the state's test.

The next class in the sequence (Defensive Pistol Skills 1) focuses on teaching the drawstroke and the skills required for the 3 yard portion of the test. Defensive Pistol Skills 2 and 3 emphasize the 7 yard shooting, gun manipulation, and one handed shooting skills, while adding the requirement that the test be shot from concealment. The four Defensive Pistol Skills courses (Essentials, 1, 2 and 3) combined, take about 18 hours to complete and are equivalent to the typical 2 day defensive pistol course taught by traveling trainers.

The sections of the test that students find the most difficult are the one handed strings shot from the 7 yard line, usually because they fail to get acceptable hits. The other section that challenges students is the 3 shots in 3 seconds at 3 yards part, because their concealment draw speed may be slow enough that they do not have enough time to fire the 2nd and 3rd shots.

Three Seconds Or Less
Any ready position **not** "full extension, aimed at target"
Start with 10 rounds in the gun (9 in magazine, 1 in chamber).
A second magazine of 10 or more is needed.
Lower capacity guns start with 5 rounds in the gun (4 +1).
20 rounds total required for this course of fire.

SCORING: use KRT-2 gray zone. Can also use IDPA target 0 rings, USPSA target (torso A and head box) or F.A.S.T. target.

LEVEL 1: 13 hits in body, 1 in head, total of 14 or more to pass
LEVEL 2: 14 hits in body, 2 in the head, total 16 or more to pass
LEVEL 3: 15 hits in body, 3 in the head, total 18 or more to pass
100%: 16 hits in body, 4 hits in the head, total of 20.

YARDS	START POSITION / INSTRUCTIONS
3	Hands at sides, gun concealed. **Step left**, draw and fire **3 body** shots, **2 handed**. (after) Holster, step right.
	Firing hand on gun, support hand on chest. Draw and fire **2 head** shots, **2 handed**.
	RELOAD OR VERIFY THAT GUN HAS 5 AND ONLY 5 ROUNDS, HOLSTER
	Hands at sides, gun concealed. **Step right**, draw and fire **3 body** shots, **2 handed**. (after) Holster, step left.
	Take one step forward (2 yards), firing hand on gun, support hand on chest. Draw and fire **2 body** shots, **firing hand only**, while backing up.
	(after) UNLOAD GUN, LOCK SLIDE, HOLSTER GUN WITH SLIDE LOCKED, MOVE TO 7 YARD LINE
7	Start with magazine in support hand, slide-locked gun in firing hand. Magazine 1"-2" from mag well, ready to insert to complete the load. On signal, insert mag, rack slide, fire **1 body** shot, **2 handed**. (after) Return to ready position.
	Ready, finger off trigger. Fire **2 head** shots, **2 handed**. (after) Holster.
	Firing hand on gun, support hand on chest. Fire 2 body shots, firing hand only.
	RELOAD OR VERIFY THAT GUN HAS AT LEAST 5 ROUNDS
	Face 90° to the left (*LH shooters, face right*), hand on gun. Turn, draw and fire **3 body** shots, **2 handed**. (after) Transfer gun to support hand.
	Firing hand on chest, gun in support hand, aimed at target, finger **OFF** trigger. Fire 2 body shots, support hand only. (after) Transfer gun to firing hand, unload/reload and holster.

Chapter 23
Calculating Par Time Drill Difficulty Level

If you want to improve, you should be running specific drills in practice, and tracking your scores. Most shooting drills are defined by these parameters:

Time
Number of Shots
Target Size
Target Distance
Scoring Method
Technique

A number of top shooters and trainers, including Bill Rogers, Greg Hamilton, Matt Burkett, Brian Enos, and Ben Stoeger, have published data that break down skills into individual parts and define the time it would take for a top shooter to perform that skill. Over the past 30 years, dozens of classification courses of fire have been written and tested in USPSA (IPSC) style competition, and data exists for many of them, showing what the best recorded scores are. From that data and review of the best scores recorded by top shooters on standard drills like the F.A.S.T. drill and El Presidente, I (Karl) made this chart of "typical" 100% Grand Master level times.

SKILL	3 yards	7 yards	15 yards	25 yards
From ready position	0.70	0.85	1.00	1.30
Open carry draw	0.80	1.00	1.25	1.50
Concealment/retention holster draw	1.10	1.30	1.50	1.80
Split time (2 shots)	0.15	0.20	0.25	0.40
Split time (one handed)	0.30	0.40	0.50	0.60
Bill Drill (draw and shoot 6)	1.60	2.00	2.50	3.50
Transition time (target to target)	0.20	0.25	0.35	0.50
Speed reload	1.0	1.25	1.50	2.00
Slide lock reload	1.5	1.75	2.00	2.25

As of this writing there are shooters that have ability as high as 120% of some of the scores used as the 100% boundaries. One example is the F.A.S.T. drill. The record on the drill is under 4 seconds, but 5 seconds (with no penalties) from concealment is widely considered to be a top tier goal. Subsequently, these numbers aren't the absolute fastest someone can (or has) performed these skills, and the values used for the 100% level are not the limits of human performance. Average performance has actually increased over the past decade. In 2018 USPSA raised the 100% levels for many classifiers.

This assumes shots are hitting the 8" circular Zero-Ring of the IDPA target or the 6.5"x11" rectangular A-zone of the Metric (original) USPSA target. For concealment draw or use of a retention holster, add 0.50 second to the draw time.

If the drill isn't shot on one of those targets, here are some comparisons of the target area of widely used targets.

TARGET	ZONE	Surface Area (sq. in.)
Dot Torture	2" circle	3.2
KRT-2	White head box – 3"-4" x 2"	7.0
USPSA Metric	Upper A Zone – 2" x 4"	8.0
NRA B 8	10 ring 3.36" circle	8.9
FBI QIT-99	Inner head box – 3"x3"	9.0
IDPA	Upper Down Zero Zone – 4" circle	12.6

TARGET	ZONE	Surface Area (sq. in.)
RM-Q	Head circle 4"	12.6
IALEFI-Q	Head circle 4"	12.6
F.A.S.T.	Head box 3" x 5"	15.0
KRT-2	White Center Zone – 3"-4"x 5"	17.5
NRA B-8	Black (9 ring) – 5.5" circle	23.8
KRT-2	Gray head – 5.5" circle	23.8
Five by Five	5" circle	25.0
B-27	10 ring - 4.25" x 6"	25.5
FBI QIT-99	Inner body box - 4" x 6.5"	26.0
USPSA Metric	Upper C Zone – 6" x 6"	36.0
IDPA	Upper -1 Zone – 6" x 6"	36.0
FBI QIT-99	Head – 6"x6"	36.0
IALEFI-Q	Bottle (head) - 6"x6"	36.0
KRT-2	Gray center zone – 6"-8"x7"	49.0
IDPA	Center Zero Ring – 8" circle	50.0
NRA B-8	8 ring – 8" circle	50.3
NRA D-1	Inner ring – 8" circle	50.3
F.A.S.T.	Body circle – 8" circle	50.3
RM-Q	Inner circle 8"	50.3
IALEFI-Q	Inner circle - 8" circle	50.3
USPSA Classic	A - 12.80" x 6"-2" trapezoid	55.0
TQ-15	Head 7"x9"	63.0
USPSA Metric	Center A Zone - 6.5" x 11"	71.5
IALEFI-Q	Outer circle = 10" circle	78.5
B-27	9 ring – 7.75" x 11.5" oval	89.1
TQ-15	Inner Chest rectangle 9.25" x 10.5"	97.1
NRA D-1	Outer ring – 12" circle	113.0
USPSA Classic	C = 17" x 6"-12" trapezoid	160.0
FBI QIT-99	"Chest" part of the bottle – 12"x15"	180.0
USPSA Metric	Center C Zone – 12" x 16"	192.0
IDPA	"Down 1" zone – 12"x16"	192.0
B-27	8 ring – 11.5" x 17.5 oval	201.0
TQ-15	Outer Chest rectangle 14" x 16"	224.0
FBI QIT-99	Full Chest (old target) = 12" x 20"	240.0

TARGET	ZONE	Surface Area (sq. in.)
IALEFI–Q	Bottle (body) 12"x22"	264.0
RM–Q	Bottle (body) 12"x22"	264.0
USPSA Classic	D – 18" x 22" – 2x 7.5x6	310.0
USPSA Metric	D Zone – 18" x 19"	342.0
IDPA	"Down 3" zone – 18" x 19"	342.0
TQ–15	Torso 19" x 24"	456.0

Disclaimer: When targets had rectangles with rounded corners, I (Karl) approximated the surface area by treating them as a rectangle. For targets with particularly complex shapes, including IPSC, USPSA, IDPA and the various torso outlines of the law enforcement targets (B–27, all the "Q"–based targets, etc.), I approximated starting with a rectangular or trapezoidal shape based on the widest and narrowest parts. Any reader who puts in the effort to calculate the exact surface area is invited to share your data with me, and I'll include it in an updated edition of the book, with attribution. For my purposes of rough comparison, these approximations are acceptable.

This data can be used to calculate what level of shooting is required to shoot a perfect score on any par time shooting drill. Break the string down into component parts and add up the totals. The difficulty, per string, is the ratio of the GM speed to the par time.

A few rules of thumb you can use are: head shots are like hitting the torso at double the distance. One handed split times are often twice as long as two handed split times regardless of distance. Those are observations based on my own training and analyzing a lot of courses of fire.

How accurate your estimate is depends on how much work you want to do trying to scale and interpolate. An example of how to do that, for those who are interested:

Ken Hackathorn's "The Test" is 10 shots in 10 seconds on an NRA B–8 target. To shoot a perfect score of 100 points requires hitting a 3.36" circle at 10 yards. The 3.36" circle simulates an 8.4" circle at 25 yards (3.36 x 2.5). So it's a Bill Drill (draw and fire 6) with 4 more shots. Since we know draw time and split times at 25 yards for the 8" circle, we can calculate the 100% "par time", which is 1.5 (draw) + 9 more shots with

0.5 splits, or 1.5 + 4.5 = 6.0 sec. Compared to the published par time of 10 seconds that indicates it takes skill about 60% of GM (6/10) to shoot a perfect score on it.

There are a lot of "loose" factors in this type of analysis, and my own belief is that this process will get you close, within 10% or so, of the actual difficulty. My own experience and observation shooting that drill is that it's a bit harder than 60% – probably 65-70%. This is where my use of approximations introduces error. This approach will get you close for a relative comparison and should not be considered as absolutes.

Example #1: Texas License To Carry test

String	Reps	Par Time	GM speed	Difficulty
1 shot from ready, 3 yards	5	2.0	0.70	35%
2 shots from ready, 3 yards	5	3.0	0.85 (0.70 + 0.15)	28%
5 shots from ready, 3 yards	1	10.0	1.30 (0.70 + 4 * 0.15)	13%
5 shots from ready, 7 yards	1	10.0	1.65 (0.85 + 4 * 0.20)	16%
1 shot from ready, 7 yards	5	3.0	0.85	28%
2 shots from ready, 7 yards	1	4.0	1.05 (0.85 + 0.20)	26%
3 shots from ready, 7 yards	1	6.0	1.25 (0.85 + 2*0.20)	21%
5 shots from ready, 7 yards	1	15.0	1.65 (0.85 + 4 *0.20)	11%
2 shots from ready, 15 yards	1	6.0	1.25 (1.00 + 0.25)	21%
3 shots from ready, 15 yards	1	9.0	1.50 (1.00 + 2*0.25)	17%
5 shots from ready, 15 yards	1	15.0	2.00 (1.00 + 4 *0.25)	13%

To calculate the total difficulty level of the drill, add up all the times for the strings, including all the repetitions. For the Texas LTC test, total time is 115 seconds. Total "GM speed" time is 23.65 seconds, for a total drill difficulty score of 20.5%. That means that someone who shoots a perfect score on the Texas LTC test has 20% of the skill of the best shooters on the planet. Someone that only 70% of the points on the test, which is a passing score, is actually at the 14% level.

Example #2: NRA Defensive Pistol Qualification

This course of fire is used in the recently developed NRA Defensive Pistol course. All drills are shot from concealment. For the 5 yard drills, the times will be estimated to be halfway between the 3- and 7- yard times. For the 10 yard drills, times are estimated to be halfway between the 7- and 15- yard times. "Tap rack" is estimated to be about the same as a reload.

String	Reps	Par Time	GM speed	Difficulty
2 shots, 3 yards	1	4.0	1.25 (1.1 + 0.15)	31%
3 shots, 5 yards	1	4.5	1.56 (1.2 + 0.18*2)	35%
3 shots, 7 yards	1	5.0	1.90 (1.5 + 0.20*2)	38%
5 shots, 10 yards	2	12.0	2.28 (1.4 + 4*0.22)	19%
1 reload 2, 5 yards	1	8.0	2.55 (1.3 + 1.25)	32%
2 reload 2, 7 yards	1	10.0	2.95 (1.3 + 0.20 + 1.25 + 0.2)	29%
3 reload 4, 7 yards	1	15.0	4.55 (1.3 + 0.20*2 + 1.25 + 3*0.20)	30%
1 tap rack 1, 7 yards	1	6.0	2.55 (1.3 + 1.25)	42%

Total par time 76.5 seconds, GM time 21.87, total drill difficulty level: 28.6%
For those designing qualification courses of fire, this type of analysis can be very useful. In this example, the relative difficulty level of each string varies from 19% to 42%.

STRATEGIES AND STANDARDS FOR DEFENSIVE HANDGUN TRAINING

Example #3: FBI Qualification Test (2000's)

String	Reps	Par Time	GM speed	Difficulty
3 shots, 3 yards, strong hand	2	3.0	1.7 (1.1 + 0.30 + 0.3)	56%
3 shots, 3 yards strong hand, switch hands, 3 rounds support hand only	1	8.0	3.95 (1.1 + 0.30 + 0.30 + 1.1*1.5 + 0.30 + 0.3)	49%
3 shots, 5 yards	4	3.0	1.56 (1.20 + .18 +.18)	52%
4 shots, 7 yards	2	4.0	1.90 (1.3 + 0.20*3)	47%
4 reload 4, 7 yards	1	8.0	3.75 (1.3 + 0.20*3 + 1.25 + 0.20*3)	47%
3 shots, 15 yards	2	6.0	2.00 (1.50 + 2 *0.25)	33%
4 shots, 15 yards	1	8.0	2.25 (1.50 + 3*0.25)	28%
move to cover, 2 standing, kneel, 3 kneeling, 25 yards	2	15.0	*5 seconds	33%

The estimate for the final string includes many skills not in our building block matrix. Transition time to transfer from one hand to the other is estimated to be 1.5x draw time. Generally the gap between top shooters and less skilled shooters increases significantly at longer range. A charitable estimate of what a GM level shooter would take for the 25 yard string is 5 seconds, based on the relative difficulty of the 15 yard strings (33 and 28%).

Exempting the 25 yard string, the total time comparison is 62 seconds (par times) vs. 27.53 = 44%

Example #4 Fundamentals of Accuracy and Speed Test (F.A.S.T.)

The F.A.S.T. drill is a simple, well known drill consisting of these steps

1) From concealment, draw and fire 2 shots at a 3"x5" box at 7 yards
2) Slide lock reload
3) 4 shots into an 8" circle at 7 yards

Using my numbers, a GM time on this drill would be:

- 1.5 sec concealment draw, (use 15 yard time for small box at 7 yards)
- 0.25 split time (15 yard split time)
- 1.75 slide lock reload to first shot on 8" circle
- 0.20 * 3 (split times for remaining shots)
- TOTAL = 1.5 + 0.25 + 1.75 + 0.60 = 4.1 seconds
-

The fastest time recorded (as of the publication of this edition) is a 3.56 from Robert Vogel, but several GM level shooters have videos on YouTube showing them running 4 second F.A.S.T. drills. That means shooting a sub 5 second F.A.S.T., which is the boundary for "Expert" set by the drill's creator, equates to roughly IPSC Master level shooting, around 80–85%.

Shooting the F.A.S.T. drill and calculating your total time (raw time plus time penalties for missed shots), and dividing 4 by your time will give you a rough idea of your basic skill level relative to an IPSC GM.

The F.A.S.T. (Fundamentals, Accuracy, & Speed Test):
Range: 7 yards
Start position: weapon concealed or in retention duty holster with all retention devices active; shooter facing downrange in relaxed stance with arms down at sides.

Drill begins from the holster, pistol loaded with exactly two rounds.

- draw
- fire two (and only two) rounds at the 3×5 box
- perform a slidelock reload
- fire four (and only four) rounds at the 8" circle

Scoring:
Open-top retention (ALS, SERPA) without concealment add 0.50 seconds to the final score.
Flap/retention mag pouch subtract 0.50 seconds.
Misses to 3x5 box add 2.00 seconds per miss.
Misses to 8" circle add 1.00 seconds per miss.

Ranking:
10+ seconds: Novice
less than 10 seconds: Intermediate
less than 7 seconds: Advanced
less than 5 seconds: Expert

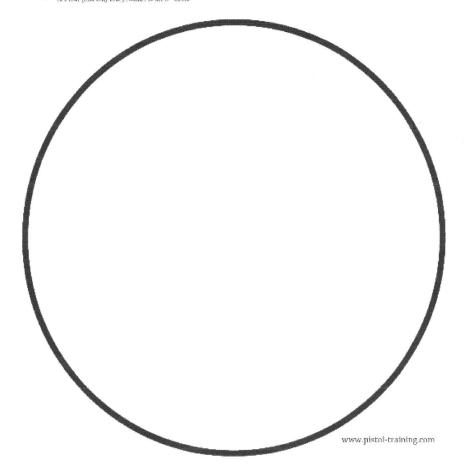

www.pistol-training.com

Karl Rehn & John Daub

Example #5 El Presidente

Range: 10 yards
Target: three IPSC targets spaced 1 yard from each other shoulder to shoulder
Start position: back to targets, hands above shoulders ("surrender position"),
Pistol: concealed, holstered
Rounds fired: 12

At the start signal, turn, then draw and fire two rounds at each of the three targets. Perform a reload, then fire two rounds at each target again. There should be four hits on each target for a total of twelve.
The classic standard was to perform the drill in under ten seconds with all A-zone hits. Any run with less than 12 A-zone hits was a failure.

Analysis:

Turning draw: 1.25 second (use 15 yard draw time)
Split: 0.22 second
Transition: 0.30 second
Split: 0.22 second
Transition: 0.30 second
Split: 0.22 second
Reload: 1.35 second (interpolate between 7 and 15 yards)
Split: 0.22 second
Transition: 0.30 second
Split: 0.22 second
Transition: 0.30 second
Split: 0.22 second
4.9 seconds total

There are some GM level shooters who have been recorded shooting El Presidente in the low 4's, but a sub-5-second El Pres is generally considered GM level shooting. For many years, 60 points in 6 seconds (a "10 factor" in Comstock points-over-time scoring) was the 100% standard for that USPSA classifier.

Example #6: Three Seconds or Less

156

Now that you get the idea, here are the results from a breakdown of our "Three Seconds or Less" test. The goal was to balance out the work to be done on each string to be roughly 50% of GM for each part. I had the opportunity to have USPSA national champion Ben Stoeger run the test in 2018, and his performance per string was within a few tenths, plus or minus, of the estimate.

String	Par Time	GM speed	Difficulty
3 yards, step, draw, shoot 3	3.0	1.4	47%
3 yards, draw & fire 2 head shots	3.0	1.5	50%
3 yards, step, draw, shoot 3	3.0	1.4	47%
2–3 yards, strong hand, 2 shots moving	3.0	1.4	47%
7 yards, partial slide lock reload, 1 shot	3.0	1.5	50%
7 yards, ready, 2 head shots	3.0	1.7	57%
7 yards, partial draw, strong hand, 2 shots	3.0	1.4	47%
7 yards, turning draw, 3 shots	3.0	1.6	53%
7 yards, weak hand, 2 shots	3.0	1.4	47%
TOTAL TIME	27.0	13.3	49%

If you cut the par time for each string down to 2.5 seconds, that raises the difficulty to 59%. With a 2.0 par for each string, the difficulty increases to 74%.

The Big Picture

I've calculated the factors for a lot of different courses of fire. A few general trends are apparent:

Your average carry permit holder, with no training beyond a state LTC course or NRA Basic course, has 20% or less of the speed and accuracy of a GM level competitor. That level is far below realistic minimum standards created by studying the tasks, speed and accuracy needed in the typical defensive pistol incident.

If the average skill level of 99% of armed citizens is below a realistic minimum, how do so many untrained/undertrained people prevail in armed self-defense incidents? In most defensive gun uses (law enforcement and citizen), presentation of the gun and threat of deadly force, with no shots fired, is sufficient to stop the threat. In others, if shots are fired, only the defender shoots. Actual gunfights (where both sides shoot) occur far less often than one-way shootings. When shots are fired, the most common reaction observed, if you study videos of actual incidents, is that people run. So in many situations shots may be fired that miss completely, or cause minor wounds, but the psychological effect of the incoming gunfire on the threat is sufficient to end the encounter. The minimum competency level becomes a much more important factor when attackers undeterred by psychological stops, particularly those capable and willing to shoot back, are involved.

Readers who are currently at that "state carry permit class" level of skill shouldn't stop carrying as a result of learning that their skills might not be to our standards. Simply having the gun and the willingness to use it, as a last resort when no other options are available and death or serious bodily injury is imminent, is preferable to going unarmed. Having the gun and the willingness to use it, and the confidence that comes from developing, and maintaining, skills at realistic minimum competency level or higher, should be the goal.

Graduates of 2-5 day pistol schools, and law enforcement officer standards are generally in the 30-50% range, with skill levels higher immediately after training is completed, diminishing over time, particularly if re-qualification or repetition of those skills only occurs 1-2 times a year.

Untimed, unstructured target practice is not the same as practicing the drills run in the training, particularly if the practice does not include evaluation of current skill level via any kind of scored drill compared to a standard or goal score.

The standards many in the private sector training community consider a realistic level of "minimum competency" are higher: in the 50-60% range.

Reaching that skill level initially requires 24-40 hours of training for the average person. Maintaining that level of skill typically requires some kind of monthly live fire practice, such as shooting an IDPA or USPSA match, or running any of the scored drills we've discussed in this book.

Most instructor certification programs run by private sector schools and law enforcement programs require shooting in the 60-75% level.

Past 60%, improvements take more time and effort, with more frequent dry and live fire practice. Typically it requires the individual to learn how to be their own coach, planning practice sessions and evaluating performance. Those are skills instructors need to develop to be competent at teaching others, and skills the vast majority of graduates of the mass-market, low-tier instructor training programs lack, and do not learn in much depth during their instructor training.

The IDPA "Master" rating is equivalent to shooting at the 65-70% level, compared to the IPSC/USPSA Master rating, which requires shooting at the 85% level.

•

Both standards have value as benchmarks of shooter skill, but outside of very serious students of defensive pistol, the use of the term "Master" by both organizations to represent disparate levels of skill confuses and misleads many who consider the two Master ratings as equal. In reality, progressing from 65% to 85% is a steep curve, with each few percent improvement taking longer and more effort to develop.

Past the 75% level of skill is generally the domain of those with very high motivation, often those competing at state, national or world levels, or those who pursue that level purely for the personal satisfaction of chasing and attaining that goal.

Almost every drill in this book can be shot with a perfect score, at a fast-enough pace, by someone who reaches the 75% level. Does the additional skill above the 75% level make any significant difference in the likely outcome of a defensive pistol incident? There's no data or analysis indicating that it does. Those who look at defensive pistol training as part of a broader program of preparedness for personal defense would likely be better off spending time developing a wider range of skills (unarmed, medical, legal, etc.) than neglecting those topics in favor of moving from 75% to 85% or higher level.

It takes a lot of work to reach the 100% level and even more work to maintain it. I can push my level up by daily dry fire and multiple live fire sessions a week. If I cut back that level of effort to once a week live fire and maybe 1-2 dry fire sessions a week, I quickly drop back to 85-90%. If the only shooting I'm doing are occasional demos during classes and I do no dry fire work, I can backslide into the 75-80% range until I go put in the work to climb back up the hill again. That slope from 75 to 100 is not only steep, it's slippery and easy to slide down.

Chapter 24
The Training and Skills Continuum

Over the past decade or so, many in the shooting and training community have thought about all the different standards and drills, and the development path to mastery. This chart was created by John Hearne of Rangemaster. It combines some of the ideas from the previous chapter (relative difficulty of shooting drills) with the concept of *automaticity*. A simple definition of automaticity is the ability to perform task without thinking about all the steps or details required.

•

It references a few drills and terms not yet discussed in this book. "POST qual" refers to the typical Peace Officer Standards and Training law enforcement qualification course of fire. "Clean El Pres" means a run on the El Presidente drill with all A zone or Zero Down hits and no penalties. "FAM" is an abbreviation for the Federal Air Marshal qualification course of fire, which can be found online. The Casino Drill is a drill used in classes taught by Tom Givens (and graduates of his instructor training program). The FBI Bullseye course is a older course of fire that's still in use by many agencies. We've discussed the F.A.S.T., the Bill Drill, and USPSA and IDPA rankings previously. The Failure Drill is a simple draw and fire 2 shots to the body, one to the head drill shot on any target that has body and head shapes.

From John Hearne, 2019

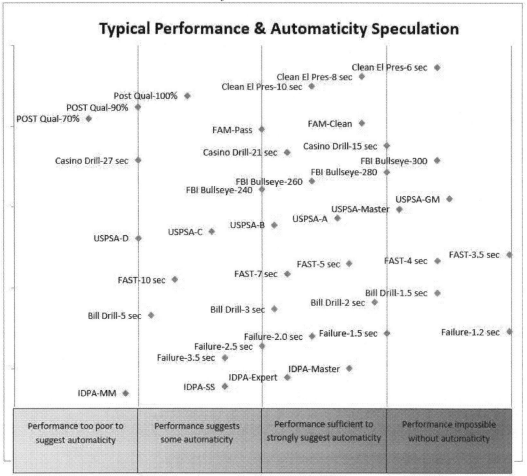

The first column of the chart covers the performance zone from 0 to 40% of GM, which includes most police academy standards. This equates to "performance too poor to suggest automaticity". That means the average cop who only shoots the qual course once or twice a year, and the state carry permit holder that only had to shoot a much simpler test once, with no annual requalification, is likely to think about the steps involved in drawing and hitting an accurate shot, if they are to succeed at it. What often occurs with those at the first level is that under stress they do not think about the steps, and with the skills not at a level where they can be performed automatically, shots miss. This is why law enforcement gunfight hit ratios are often low.

The second column spans the 40-60% skill level range. This is the level that most graduates of modern pistol schools attain by the end of the course (whether they maintain it and how long they maintain it is dependent on frequency and quality of practice). The chart authors consider this level of shooter to be capable of "some automaticity".

The third column spans the 60-90% skill level range. The level of effort required to reach those performances is significantly more. To get to the 80-90% level, at least initially, usually requires a focused program (such as those detailed in books by Ben Stoeger and Mike Seeklander). It requires effort outside of simply attending weekend classes or using local matches as 'practice'. Structured, determined practice is essential. That effort pays off by producing performance "sufficient to strongly suggest automaticity".

The final column is from 90% to that 120%+ upper echelon discussed in the previous section. To reach this level requires tremendous commitment and effort: hours a day, dozens of hours a week, tens of thousands of trigger presses (dry or live). So how much automaticity is a minimum acceptable standard?

John Hearne, in his section of the book Straight Talk on Armed Defense, uses this graphic to explain the importance of automaticity to defensive pistol skills. There are elements you can't control, and elements you can.

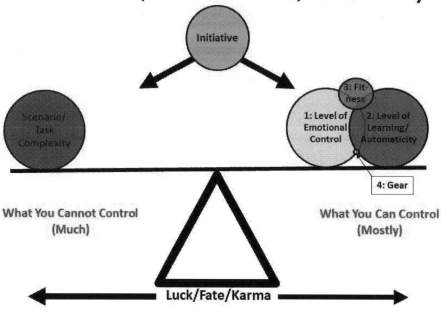

Who Wins, Who Loses, and Why

Initiative

3: Fitness

1: Level of Emotional Control

2: Level of Learning/Automaticity

Scenario/Task Complexity

4: Gear

What You Cannot Control (Much)

What You Can Control (Mostly)

◄———— Luck/Fate/Karma ————►

His concepts connect back to the previous sections of this book. Note that "gear", which was identified in Section 1 as the most popular topic of interest to shooters, is the smallest of the four elements that be controlled, because Hearne considers it the least important.

If you look at the relative sizes of the four elements as an indicator of training priorities, they translate to:

Gear – least important, but as we've noted earlier, the topic of greatest interest to the largest segment of gun owners

Desire to buy skill with gear is human nature. Nothing gets me more ugly comments on the 'mainstream' gun forums I'm active on than suggesting that someone spend their money on ammo and training instead of buying a new gun. The mainstream media attempts to equate volume of gun sales with the level of interest in firearms and shooting.

Fitness – not just being stronger, but also taking care of nutrition and sleep. Mobility and endurance.

Fitness is important on a day to day and whole life basis, and just like gear there are advantages to being tuned up. But the other two factors on Hearne's chart are the biggest ones.

Emotional control - developed from scenario based training, including force on force training and close quarters training that includes physical contact.

This is, of course, out of alignment with the majority of training offered in the private sector. The most widely attended courses are lecture courses on state laws that include extremely low stress, easy to pass shooting tests. The most popular courses beyond the state minimums are high round count skills development classes, again with limited physical or emotional stress beyond a graduation qualification live fire test.

Automaticity – developed from frequent, correct repetitions of specific skills, until they can be performed at a level likely to result in success in an actual defensive incident.

In addition to being a shooting instructor, I (Karl) am also a professional musician. In 2018 I spent about 140 days on the range teaching shooters, and I performed 147 gigs, playing keyboards and singing. A lot of the music I play is blues and jazz – styles of music where no two performances of a song are the same. The players all work from the same framework (lyrics and chords and song structure), but the number of times each section is repeated, the tempo, the phrasing, the solos, the bass line, chord voicings, and other elements can change as needed to adapt to the mood, the setting and what the other members of the band are doing.

To be able to perform at that level requires automaticity and the ability to apply fundamentals, on demand, in the moment. There's no time to say "stop while I figure out how to play a C7#9 chord with a G as the bottom note" while the song is being performed. If that was the chord & voicing that was needed at that instant, you either got it there on time, in the groove, you played it wrong and it sounded bad, or you failed to play it at all. Maybe if the song was played at 70 beats per minute that gave you enough time to keep up – but the drummer and guitar player kicked it off at 90 bpm. In that situation you didn't have the minimum skills to deal with the situation. And that part of the situation wasn't under your control.

Music skills progress from basics like learning what key makes what note, to putting them together in scales, to playing scales in rhythm, to playing scale patterns, to copying other people's solos, to making up your own solos "in the moment" at home, to doing that in front of people...in a situation where you either succeed, fail or forfeit.

As your skills become more and more advanced, the amount of automaticity increases. Depending on the (musical) situation, that either results in more high level brain functions being available for other tasks (creative ideas, for example), or simply allows the subconscious mind to do all the work, processing and acting faster (and often better) than conscious thought. I've had jazz musicians and top level competitive shooters both talk about having moments where they were simply "watching the movie" or "listening to the song" as everything was happening at the autonomous level.

Automaticity doesn't mean that someone is simply running a rote program that can't be stopped or altered. There's a subset of firearms trainers who have a sincere but incorrect and unproven belief that practicing 'range choreography' or spending excessive time getting good at a pre-programmed timed drill will result in that rote behavior occurring during an actual incident, when it may be the wrong thing to do. My observation is that none of the trainers who hold that belief have ever developed their own skills at any task far enough that they really understand what automaticity is or how it's applied.

There are guitar players capable of playing scale patterns at speeds so fast that the individual notes cannot be discerned. That skill came from endless hours practicing those scale patterns. Yet onstage, in front of thousands of people, under stress to create a 16 bar solo "in the moment", none of them revert to playing their finger dexterity exercises for the entire solo. Elements of the drills are broken apart and used as needed.

I've run many competition shooters, from a wide variety of shooting games, in force on force scenarios. They may act like a guitar player in a rock band sitting in with a jazz group: using the skills they have as best they can only to discover gaps their background didn't prepare them for. Those who only do live fire training don't have many skills related to reading pre-fight cues, communication or any other aspect of human interaction, but if the scenario gets to the part where it's time to move, draw and shoot – they have that part down and do just fine with it, like a guitar player set loose on a 12 bar blues in E.

Many famous gunfighters and shootists shot competition – many back in the era when competitions consisted of exactly the same course of fire over and over again. Charles Askins, Bill Jordan, and Jim Cirillo shot bullseye and Police Pistol Combat (PPC) matches, for example. In the modern era both USPSA and IDPA matches require a skill absent from those earlier gun games: the ability to look at a complex course of fire, given limited time, visualize a plan, and then do the mental work to program that plan deeply enough that execution of that plan occurs at maximum speed with perfect accuracy, on the first attempt. Competition critics point out that in actual incidents, the exact positions of the "shoot" and "don't shoot" targets are not known, and the targets move and shoot back. That's all true – but SWAT teams and others planning military assaults and raids use visualization to make the best plan they can, in the limited time they have, and then adapt as needed once the go signal is given.

Competition doesn't teach the "in the moment" adaptation as well as scenario based training does, but it builds a skill that older pistol sports do not. I'm unaware of any critic of modern pistol competition that's actually put in the time to develop that mental skill and apply it during a match. Anyone who has shot some misses on steel targets that forced an unexpected reload, particularly on stages that involve swingers and other moving targets, understands that simply having started a plan intending it run autonomously doesn't mean that you can't adapt it in the moment. Those at the extreme high level of skill can even automate some corrective actions. On Steel Challenge stages, the typical low to medium skill shooter waits to hear the "ding' from the hit plate before moving the gun to the next target. The medium-to-high skill shooter will fire and immediately start moving the gun to the next target. If the shot missed (and was noticed because there was no ding), that level of shooter will have to bring the gun back to the missed target and shoot at it again. At the highest level, the fastest shooters are "calling" their shots as good or bad and making the (autonomous) decision to re-engage it, before the gun has finished recoiling from the missed shot, while the gun is still on the missed target. So even decision making itself can be pushed to the autonomous level with enough repetitions of correct practice.

Some observations about automaticity: I started early in music. Piano lessons at 5, guitar lessons at 7. I worked hard at both and was equally skilled at both until 6th grade, when I learned French horn to be in school band. I had to split time between 3 instruments through the end of high school. During that time the skills of playing those instruments were all developed to a reasonable level of automaticity. I quit playing French horn at 18, and actually sold my horn to buy the 1911 .45 I started shooting USPSA matches with when I was 24. I played less and less guitar over the years but still pick one up a few times a year. I play piano at least every other day, and on days when I play gigs, I'm playing 2-4 hours at a time. Ben Stoeger once commented that he got from unclassified to GM in less than a year, and then it took him 5 more years to win his first national championship. That's useful perspective on the slope of the learning curve to that highest level of performance and automaticity.

The farther you push your skills into automaticity, the longer they will be retained, and the losses in performance level will be slower to fade. However: they will fade. I have recordings of myself playing finger picked acoustic guitar pieces that were, at the time, fully autonomous. 30 years later, I would have to re-learn them. The re-learning process would not take the same time it took to learn them originally, but because of the gap in usage of that skill, it would take some time. The last time I picked up a trumpet (basically the same as a French horn), my abilities were poor at best. Similarly, one summer many years ago I got serious about skeet and was shooting shotgun 2-3 days a week for months. It would probably take me several weeks of that level of practice to get back to where I was, or longer if the frequency of practice was less. Each summer I knock the dust off of my USPSA competition gear and shoot some local matches. It usually takes me weeks of daily dry fire and 2-3 days a week of live fire practice to actually shoot like the GM my classification card says I am. Don't assume because you reached a particular level once, for a short period, that the skill is available at that level if you don't maintain it. But the good news is that it won't take as long to get back to that peak level the second time around, and if you train past the level you can live with as a maintenance level, you can keep that with less intense and less frequent practice than it took to achieve the peak.

Chapter 25
Drills, Qualifications, Standards and Tests

In April 2015, I, John, began assembling a collection of live fire defensive-oriented pistol drills important to me and my goals. I added drills as I encountered them, including after taking classes from trainers such as Tom Givens, Gabe White, Spencer Keepers, Brian Hill, and Massad Ayoob – and of course, Karl.

Originating in the December 24, 2017 episode of the Handgun World Podcast (episode 443), then presented in this book, is a collection of drills Karl and I selected as training standards for defensive handgun shooting. April 2020, Karl asked me to send him a couple drills he knew I had on record, so I sent him the file of my rough collection. I don't believe I had ever shared my collection with anyone – it was always just by me for me. However, seeing how well received our book, especially the Drills section, has been received, I decided to clean up my collection and share it publicly.

The eBook *Drills, Qualifications, Standards, & Tests* was publicly released on the krtraining.com website in March 2021. It's a collection, easily kept on your phone for field reference, of over 60 drills and variations to help you build confidence through competence

While this started as a collection for me, it's grown into something more since the release of this book. I've added some drills to capture a moment in time, be it a unique match or a part of gun culture legacy. I also found this to be an appropriate venue for deeper exploration into the topic of minimum competency, including developing a course of fire that could provide you with a meaningful assessment in your personal journey of self-improvement (see the *Minimum Competency Assessment* in this book).

Strictly speaking, most of the eBook's contents are not drills but rather qualifications, standards, tests, and other measures of skill and performance; I'll refer to them as "drills" for simplicity in communication (but there's a reason the title is an enumeration).

I originally chose these drills to help me ensure competency and confidence in myself in areas I believe are important for defensive pistol use. While it's important to define and meet minimum competency, I want my own skills to exceed the minimum – I expect you do, too. I find drills such as these to be challenging, and I believe constant work on them and their underlying skills help maintain and grow one's abilities. Furthermore, they are quantifiable, repeatable, trackable, and thus allow for measurement and determination of progression – especially in areas that need improvement.

By no means is this a static set of drills, a set of the only things one should practice, or any sort of be–all–end–all. Really, it came down to wanting a simple, single document containing things I find value in running and referencing. It makes it easy for me to keep a PDF on my phone. If I don't know what to do at the range, I can open this file, pick something, and shoot it as my cold opener. It will reveal some weakness I can then work on during the practice session.

The *Drills, Qualifications, Standards, & Tests* eBook will be periodically updated. May 2022 saw a significant update as the place where I first published the *Minimum Competency Assessment*. Sign up on the KR Training mailing list to receive notifications of updates. Thank you for downloading, reading, and sharing it with your friends.

Chapter 26
Minimum Competency Assessment

Target: Preferred: KRT-2 (only white/gray areas).
Alternates: IDPA (only -0 rings), IPSC Metric (only A & B zones),
RFTS-Q (only 8" and 4" rings), IALEFI-Q's (only 8", 4" rings).

Gear: Shoot it with the gear you carry in public, not range-only training gear. If possible, shoot your carry ammo. 25 rounds.

All shooting is freestyle unless otherwise noted. For "hands on phone", use a prop phone (e.g. empty ammo box/tray) and hold it the way you most commonly interact with your phone (held to your ear to talk, two-hands in front while texting, etc.). Drop the phone on the signal. For "hands in fence" your hands should be forward in the "I don't want any trouble here" position. When side-stepping, make one meaningful step either left or right; doesn't matter which direction, but consider switching up throughout the assessment.

10 yards
Hands at sides. Draw and fire 2 to the body in 4.0 seconds

7 yards
Hands at sides. Draw and fire 3 to the body in 4.0 seconds
Hands in fence. Draw and fire 1 to the body in 2.5 seconds
Hands on phone. Draw and fire 1 to the body in 2.5 seconds

5 yards
Hands at sides. Side-step, draw and fire 1 to the body in 2.5 seconds
Hands in fence. Side-step, draw and fire 1 to the body in 2.5 seconds
Hands on phone. Side-step, draw and fire 1 to the body in 2.5 seconds
Hands at sides. Side-step, draw and fire 3 to the body in 3.5 seconds
Hands at sides. Side-step, draw and fire 2 body, 1 head in 4.0 seconds

3 yards
Hands at sides. Side-step, draw and fire 1 to the body in 2.0 seconds
Hands in fence. Side-step, draw and fire 1 to the body in 2.0 seconds
Hands on phone. Side-step, draw and fire 1 to the body in 2.0 seconds
Hands at sides. Side-step, draw and fire 3 to the body in 3.0 seconds
Hands at sides. Side-step, draw and fire 2 body, 1 head in 3.5 seconds
(Total of 25 rounds)

Karl Rehn & John Daub

Scoring

Count the hits. 1 point for an acceptable hit; 0 points for an unacceptable hit, including shots over time, shots not fired.
23 of 25 acceptable hits (92%) to pass. Safety violations result in failure.

Variations

- Ignore the side step; ignore the start positions
- If you are having trouble making the par time and points, try starting hands at sides (no fence, no phone) and/or try standing still (no side-step).
- These add task complexity, so simplifying the strings may help you in achieving the times and points.
- In time, work to add these back in.
- Reduce par times
- Try a 0.5 second reduction across the board.
- Try a 1.0 second reduction across the board.
- Smaller target zones
- On the KRT-2, use only the white trapezoids.
- On another target, perhaps a 6" circle and a horizontal 3x5 card.
- Use shootsteel.com cardboard training targets, just A and B zones.
- All body shots become head shots, all head shots into something smaller (e.g. on the KRT-2, the A or B 2" circles)
- Hit factor scoring
- I don't think this assessment lends to hit factor scoring. However, you could record your time for each individual string/concept and work to beat those times.

Note: you can pick one variation, you can pick multiple (e.g. 0.5 second par time reduction, with body shots becoming head shots and head the 2" circles). If you were to pick a single way to make it more challenging, start by shooting the assessment as-written but using smaller target zones. **Make acceptable hits.**

Chapter 27
Analysis of the Minimum Competency Assessment

Evolution

In April 2021, Claude Werner wrote about the importance of the first shot. While not groundbreaking to Karl and me, something about Claude's presentation – especially knowing Claude's focus on beginners and competency – brought the topic into a new light. It made me think about my minimum considerations: might the floor actually be lower? That "draw to first shot" (or really, "draw to first acceptable hit") may be the actual floor? No, I don't think we can omit multiple acceptable hits, but it makes me think about the gravity of the notion of draw-to-first-acceptable-hit. Thus, one could conclude when assessing minimum competency, the assessment should focus on these six points, with an emphasis on draw-to-first-acceptable-hit.

Consider as well a post on pistol-forum.com from poster nycnoob:

> I have identified several "skills" that I think are practical and will be my personal focus this year.
>
> 1) Draw from concealment and hit a headshot (say 3x5 card). Really, if this is fast and accurate / every time, you would hardly need any other skill for a gun fight, if you miss the first shot, then things are much more difficult. Some instructors on Todd Green's board think it is important to practice more than one shot because a poor grip will often work for one shoot but not work for multiple. So practice more than one shot to ensure you are not sloppy but the real skill is a one shot head shoot... IF the above is true then perhaps the famous failure drill (two to

the body one to the head) is shot backwards.
Perhaps you should try and take the headshot first and go to the
body if you miss/can't take it.

He references HeadHunter, who is Claude Werner, when he continues
with words from Claude:

Quote:
Street Survival: Tactics For Armed Encounters
Q: What did you do wrong?
A: The biggest thing, I think, was to miss with my first shot...

The poster nycnoob goes on to say that [HeadHunter, aka Claude Werner]
talks about "after the first shot, everyone was moving and things got
much harder."

I also appreciate something my friend Kirk Clark said:

> *One of the less immediately apparent advantages of having*
> *the power of a fast, sure draw to shot, is that you are far more*
> *free to put the gun away once you have done your shooting,*
> *knowing you can quickly and reliably produce it if it becomes*
> *necessary again.*

This doesn't mean other skills such as reloads, malfunctions, longer
distances, lower strings of fire, scanning, weak-hand-only, target
transitions, movement, etc. aren't important: they're just above
minimum skills. Crawl, walk, run – let's first get people crawling (parts,
nomenclature, and basic marksmanship) to then walking upon a good
performance floor.

Aside: I am going to call it "draw to first acceptable hit" (DTFAH). Not
just because "acceptable hit" is one of my on-brand phrases, but I do
think it's more precise in describing the concept. A "shot" may imply
hitting the intended target, but it doesn't clearly state it – is a "shot" just
making noise? I would also argue that a hit anywhere on the FBI-Q bottle

target may be a hit, but that lower-left corner really isn't acceptable when one considers anatomy (that's a fat roll, not something of anatomical worth). We don't just want a "shot" or a "hit", we want an acceptable hit. Words shape our mindset.

Name

I'm calling this an **assessment**. It's not a drill, but it could be with all those draw-to-first-acceptable-hit strings. It's certainly not a qualification. And I don't want to call it a test because I'm not out to grade you. I want a means by which an individual's skills can be assessed. Where are you in your journey of (minimum) competency? Are you not there yet? Are you there? Are you beyond? This is intended as a way to assess and provide a metric, a frame of reference, a guidepost in your journey.

I fear someone may take this work – this Assessment – and want to use it as a means of codifying what is, or what should be. For example, licensure only if you can pass a standard. There is danger in that: it creates barriers, akin to a poll tax. Also, who gets to define the standard? Because for sure, I don't define minimum competency the same as others; consider the differences outlined in my original article just between myself, Karl Rehn, and Tom Givens. This is a much larger topic in and of itself. Just realize this isn't any sort of gospel, it's just a milestone in a journey and I hope it creates thought, discussion, and a desire to improve.

Equipment

The original intent of my work and thus this Assessment was focused towards private citizens. As my thoughts progressed on the topic, I realized that while private citizens are a core context for me, in the end self-defense is self-defense – law enforcement officers have the right, too. Thus, for the purposes of this Assessment, equipment is "what you carry every day". If that's a concealed AIWB Roland Special, your issued bone-stock Glock in a Safariland Level III, or a snub in your pocket – that's what you shoot. Your mode of carry should be the mode you use "on the street" – not your special range kit, not your gamer rig, not the larger gun that's easier to shoot vs. the little gun you actually carry. Shoot how and what you carry.

Ammo is one place where you can vary. Ideally, you'd shoot this with your carry ammo since many people's carry ammo is different than their practice ammo (e.g. +P with more recoil, potentially a different point-of-aim vs. point-of-impact). Thus, shooting the Assessment with your carry ammo provides knowledge and confidence in your complete carry gear. However, carry ammo is expensive, so if you wish to swap your carry ammo for practice ammo that's fine. However, if at all possible, try to shoot this Assessment with your carry ammo. One way to approach this is to shoot the Assessment as a part of ammo rotation. When you swap your old carry ammo for new ammo (on whatever schedule you perform this), use the old carry ammo to shoot this Assessment.

While this Assessment isn't necessarily about assessing hardware, it's certainly about your ability to perform with your chosen hardware. The attack doesn't consider what you are carrying and how you are carrying it. By knowing how you perform with your carry gear you can either build confidence with that gear, or determine how you need to change what gear you carry.

Target

Our context is that of self-defense; thus, we need a context-appropriate target, such as a silhouette. And not just any silhouette, but one with proper target zones accurate in both size and placement. I believe the best target is the KRT-2 – freely available to download and print from the KR Training website (be sure to print on 11x17" paper). Yes, the target is on-brand, but I do think it's an excellent representation of anatomical correctness; we explain why in our book. And again, the KRT-2 is freely available as a download and is cheaper to print than other commercial targets.

Other targets can work too. For example, the IPSC Metric (scoring just A & B Zone hits), the IDPA (scoring only -0 zone body and head hits), and the RFTS-Q (scoring the 8" and 4" circles). Targets such as these have similar intent in their design. You may not get apples-to-apples comparison, if say you shot it once on a KRT-2 then again on an IPSC Metric. But just keep things in mind and work to shoot well enough so the minutia of target differences become irrelevant.

Note there are other scoring zones on these targets, like the –3 on the IPDA or D–zone on an IPSC Metric. But those are less than ideal zones when you consider actual human anatomy. Once again, Claude Werner writing about "Why I Hate the –3 Zone":

1. The –3 zone, or the D zone of the USPSA Metric, on the sides of the target is basically where a man's arms are when they're hanging by his side. A man holding a weapon at or near eye level would not have anything there below a line approximately even with the middle of the –o zone.

2. The area of the –3 zone below the –1 zone very closely aligns with the area of the male body below the waist...

3. From about two inches above the bottom of the –o zone down to the bottom of the –1 zone corresponds generally to the area from the xyphoid process to the waist. Emergency room physicians have told me that they consider this entire area to be an abdominal wound and not nearly as serious as a wound in the torso above that line.

4. Finally, by process of elimination, the area [in the upper torso]is where all the "good stuff" is, as one physician put it to me. This is the area of the torso where a bullet has the best probability of quickly stopping a deadly threat to one's life. Note that this area goes all the way up to the neckless chin.

This is why I'm only considering hits to the high-center chest (heart & lungs) and head (ocular window) as acceptable for this context. And thus, the importance of considering anatomy in selecting an acceptable target.

This is also why I'm not considering other sorts of targets. The B-27 and B-21 are just not good when you consider anatomy and operating context. No zombie targets, no abstract shapes, no bullseyes, no targets that don't serve the purpose of a concealed carry context; they may be fine targets, just not applicable to this Assessment. That said, while the KRT-2 is preferred, I wouldn't want to see someone NOT shoot this for lack of having the KRT-2. Hopefully you can see from the recommended target and suggested alternatives what the general desire is for an acceptable target – so if what you have available is in that realm and spirit, go for it. Just realize you may not have an apples-to-apples comparison if you shoot again using a different target, but so long as when you shoot it you use the same target, you're at least able to compare your performance against your prior performance.

If you want to read an interesting and enlightening discussion about targets and correctness, give this discussion thread a read: https://pistol-forum.com/showthread.php?9306-A-Separate-Thread-For-Anatomical-Correctness-Of-Targets.

Scoring

This goes back to my notion of "unacceptable hits": either you hit what's acceptable, or you don't. Thus, scoring simply aligns with that notion: one point for acceptable hits, zero points for unacceptable hits (including not getting the shots off, or going over time). The time element is a crucial aspect to the Assessment because when you are trying to defend your life, time matters and you typically won't have a lot of it, so you have to be able to get work done in a small amount of time. The timer adds a pressure to the shooter to perform, which can be considered part of stress inoculation because again, defending your life is likely to be a high-pressure event.

I don't think this Assessment lends to hit factor scoring, which is points divided by time, aka Comstock scoring. (For example, 60 points in 10 seconds is a 6 hit factor. 60 points in 6 seconds is a much better 10 factor score.) Certainly, if you are curious for your performance you can score it that way. But as this is about minimum competency assessment, if people can pass as-written, I believe that's sufficient for the purposes of the Assessment.

Distances

From data sets such as Rangemaster, FBI, DEA, and what we've seen in many Active Self Protection videos, we know typical gunfights for the private citizen are in the 0-5 yard range. Consequently, I wanted to ensure those distances were primarily represented.

I did think about less than 3-yard distances, but I felt that ran into practical limitations. For example, muzzle blast often tears up the targets; some ranges won't or can't let you shoot < 3 yards. Also, shooting at those distances is generally done from retention, and that's arguably beyond minimum competency.

If the typical distance maxes out at 5 yards, why the 7 and 10 yards? It's a combination of the world we live in, reinforcing the application of good technique, and building confidence through challenge.

The notion of 7 and 10 yards is essentially "across a room". While most private citizen self-defense incidents happen outside the home (see: transitional spaces), many people take their first steps in gun ownership around the notion of home defense. If this is the mental frame someone comes in with, I see good in helping them build confidence in their ability to perform within that framework ("yes, I could make a shot across a room"). We can consider 10 yards to be across a larger room (open floor plans).

It could be said that based upon the data, we only need to go out to 7 yards. My thinking is going to 10 is still good. When the flag flies, you're not going to know the exact yardage to your assailant. If it's truly going to be inside of 7 yards, then 10 makes for a good margin of error. Having shot competently to 10 yards means you're primed to the notion of longer distance shots; confidence is a performance aid.

Shooting at 3 yards you can get away with not using sighted fire and still get acceptable hits. The further back you get (the smaller the target gets), the more you must refine your sight picture. I had a student in class that was nailing it at 3 yards but wild at 7. The student was not using their sights. Once the correction was applied, acceptable hits were happening at 7 yards. Having longer distances in the Assessment helps reinforce good shooting technique.

And let's face it: shooting at 10 yards can be hard and intimidating, especially for someone who is working their way up to this level. Plus, it's not just shooting at 10 yards, it's shooting cold at 10 yards. It might induce some stress, some discomfort. This is good for it is through discomfort we grow. Challenge builds confidence.

Repetition

I think Ken Hackathorn's "The Wizard" is a fantastic test – when shot cold, it's an excellent low-round count diagnostic of the most crucial of mechanical skills: Draw to Acceptable First Hit.

Setup
5 rounds – preferably with the ammunition you carry
IDPA target or equivalent; 4" head, 8" body.
From concealment – in the manner in which you normally carry a concealed weapon
No gamer or "for class" rigs.
If you are carrying in a pocket, you are allowed to start with your hand in the pocket on the gun.

All strings have a 2.5 second par time.

3 yd Draw and fire 1 head shot, strong-hand-only.
5 yd Draw and fire 1 head shot, both hands.
7 yd Draw and fire 1 head shot, both hands.
10 yd Draw and fire 2 body shots, both hands.
Note: the 5 yd string can be shot 1 or 2 hands,
but typically is shot with 2.

Scoring
Shots: 3 head, 2 body

Using an IDPA target, it is scored by the rings (-0, -1, -3).
You can drop 2 points and pass the drill.
Exceed any time limit – fail.
Miss a headshot – fail.

At its' heart you can see how my Assessment draws inspiration from it. However, I think this test lacks one crucial component: ensuring skill and not luck. Consider 5^5 (Claude Werner's emphasis on "and 5 times") or the courses of fire from the TacCon21 Match or the Rangemaster Master Instructor qualification (from our free e-book) – note the use of repetition. Repetition ensures you can actually do the thing instead of perhaps getting lucky on that one run.

In his talk, *Who Wins, Who Loses, and Why: Understanding Human Performance When Death is on the Line*, John Hearne speaks of the concept of overlearning – "Skills practiced until they can't be done wrong are overlearned." From the January 2022 slides of this lecture:

> *What We Need*
>
> *We "know" with greater certainty that higher levels of skill combined with emotional control makes everyone safer. We "know" that improving skill helps improve emotional control. We don't serve people by allowing them to sit in their own poop. We serve people by giving them the tools to do better and punish them when they don't.*
>
> *We Need – Overlearned Skills*
>
> *When we look at the literature, well developed (robust) motor programs are faster and more accurate. Faster and more accurate very directly equates to higher, not lower, shooting standards. We need to reconsider what is "good enough." Most shooting problems do not require large amounts of technical shooting skill. However, one of the best ways to make sure*

people have enough skill under stress is to make them have more in non-stress environments.

The repetition within the Assessment aids overlearning. Some people go to the range to just enjoy shooting. They enjoy selecting drills and seeing if they can shoot them (loser buys!). That's a good day to a lot of people. In designing the Assessment, it is a goal that if the only thing someone ever does is shoot 1 box (50 rounds) of ammo once a month by running this Assessment twice (or better, shoot once then use the remaining 25 rounds to practice whatever suck the Assessment run uncovered), I wanted the runs to be meaningful in contribution to their building/maintaining of their competence.

In addition to the repetition, you'll notice the Assessment has a pattern of execution – this is intentional. It's easy to detect the pattern and drop your focus and attention, thus potentially blowing some strings. It's important to stay focused on the task at hand and not let mind games, predictions, nor outcome-focus affect good process execution.

Par Times

Determining par times was the most difficult part for me: what exactly is the right performance standard?

In a seminal discussion on the topic of "what is good enough?" John Hearne examines the concepts of overlearning and automaticity (discussed earlier in this book).

I believe minimum competency requires some level of automaticity: to be able to perform the mechanical gun skills (draw, aim, press trigger, etc.) "automatically" so that your brain is freer to deal with the novel stimulus of the encounter. From John Hearne:

> *I would fully acknowledge that it is possible to have some automaticity if one isn't super fast. I would offer that it is impossible to be super fast without some degree of automaticity. I would say that lower levels of performance do*

not exclude overlearning and the resultant automaticity, but that higher levels absolutely require it (except for some genetically gifted freaks with incredible kinesthetic intelligence and eye sight)

Over the years I've observed thousands of students and seen automaticity develop in them. I can see the students are thinking less about those base mechanical skills and instead focusing on the novelty (e.g. class is teaching movement while shooting, it's the novel movement skill they are thinking about – the drawing, the shooting, is on "auto-pilot"). Matching context to the KR Training curriculum, I look at our Defensive Pistol Skills (DPS) 1, 2, and 3 classes. DPS-1 is designed as the first post-LTC class, where a student learns to draw from concealment, getting multiple hits, in a small area, from close range, quickly, using both hands. This includes shooting our Three Seconds or Less test and passing at the 70% level. By definition, students coming in to DPS-1 are not minimally competent, but should leave class with the knowledge of the skills needed (then it's up to them to put in the practice to develop them).

A prerequisite for attending DPS-2 is to pass DPS-1, meaning on paper they have the skills to be minimally competent. But do they have the automaticity? From my observations over the years, I would say that automaticity is starting to develop. The material in DPS-2 requires the student to have some degree of clue and performance in those minimal skills, especially to be able to pass Three Seconds or Less at the 80% level. You just can't do the things that DPS-2 requires if you don't have some sort of automaticity in those minimal skills. Consequently, I think this gives us some indication of a line where automaticity of these skills is starting to develop. Now how to quantify that level?

I started with Karl's outline of how to calculate drill difficulty presented in Section 3 of this book. It doesn't cover everything nor give me "plug-and-chug" numbers, but it does provide a good guideline and framework for getting in the ballpark. The calculation is ultimately looking at 100% USPSA/IPSC Grandmaster performance levels, so it must be scaled down. To what level should it be scaled?

Let's go back to the Three Seconds or Less test. Again, we use Three Seconds or Less as the graduation requirement from our Defensive Pistol

Skills 1, 2, and 3 classes: DPS-1 must pass at 70%, DPS-2 at 80%, and DPS-3 at 90%. In our book, Karl calculates shooting Three Seconds at a 90% score to be about 50% of GM skill level. Roughly speaking then, DPS-2 passing is about 40% of GM, and DPS-1 is about 35% of GM. Thus, when calculating the par times for the Assessment, I opted for about 40% of GM-level calculation – somewhere in C-class.

Being somewhere in C-class is about right. Go back to John Hearne's automaticity speculation chart. USPSA C-class is a level where some level of automaticity is starting to be developed, and that jives with the skills and desired path. If we're talking self-defense usage context, automaticity with core skills of aiming and shooting are desired, so our brain can be freed to process the novel stimulus of the particular situation we suddenly find ourselves in.

Another consideration is the 3 shots, 3 yards, 3 seconds trope. Data generally reflects this as a typical successful situation/response. If we put credence into that as perhaps the simplest metric of skill performance, it could be viewed as an anchor for all other times. You could say a breakdown is 2.0 DTFAH, 0.5 second splits.

So, with all of this I did some math, some fuzzy adjustments. I came up with the times that you see in the Assessment. On both 5 and 7 yards being 2.5 seconds, the math actually worked out to about 2.3 and 2.7. I opted to round it to 2.5 for ease of administration.

For what it's worth, in beta-testing this Assessment, I had a class of DPS-2 students shoot it as a group. Most times were made just slightly under stated par times, but a number went over. Just over half of the participants passed, with a couple just barely not making it. I've had others shoot the Assessment as well, and given what I see, I feel the selected times are good and in line with the goals of the Assessment.

Hands, Movement

I opted to put in different hand/start positions as well as movement.

We don't live with our hands by our sides. In fact, a reality of today is we are likely to have a phone in our hands when/if we are selected to be a victim. I appreciate Lee Weems' idea of an empty ammo tray as a mobile phone stand-in/prop, especially because the reaction we want to train is discarding/dropping the phone before drawing – it's easier to practice the drop with an empty tray than your $1000 phone. The Fence is a good concept to understand and incorporate into your skillset as a means of confrontation management. If you aren't familiar with The Fence, put "the fence Geoff Thompson" into your favorite Internet search engine.

Movement was added because it's a good idea. Which is better? To shoot or to not get shot? To not get shot. To "get off the X" can help you avoid getting shot. Yes, it's just a side-step, and I know some debate side steps versus more dynamic movement (e.g. run to cover). My take? This is about minimum competency – crawl, walk, run. Allow people to first crawl, taking this first (side) step towards understanding the importance of movement.

Why not always move? From my training with Tom Givens, the side-step is really only effective in close range. When you get to 7-10 yards, the angles change enough that a simple side-step won't likely take you out of the attacker's line of sight. Why not move and shoot? Not just because I learned from Paul Howe to either shoot or move, but I'd argue that is a skill beyond the minimum.

Additionally, adding in movement and hand positions adds to the cognitive load, which in time hopefully helps you build automaticity (e.g. discarding unnecessary things from your hands). That's important towards building competence.

In the Force Science News, Chris Butler writes in Firearms Training for Real-World Assaults:

> *Neurons that Fire Together, Wire Together*

> *"Hebb's Law" (Spike Timing Dependent Plasticity) is one of the most well-researched and accepted concepts in psychology and human performance. Hebb's Law informs us that motor pathways are not formed in isolation, which means the context and conditions in which the pathways are created (i.e., the training) matter.*

Take, for example, the standard draw stroke of the handgun. This serial motor program consists of multiple, individual, discrete motor movements. Officers must grip the gun, release the retention mechanisms, lift the gun from the holster, align the muzzle, drive (present) the gun towards the threat, and move the trigger finger to the trigger.

Every time an officer conducts the draw stroke, the brain's motor cortex builds stronger motor neural pathways. During this repetitive process, a type of insulation known as myelin forms around the involved neurons. This "myelination" can result in a connection that is 10x faster than unmyelinated nerves. For shooters, this high-speed connection can result in an efficient draw stroke that requires no attentional resources ("motor automaticity").

Butler asserts the other side of Hebb's Law can result in undesirable responses, saying an officer whose totality of live fire training is "stand (still) and shoot", it's likely this will myelinate a pathway to stand (still) while shooting, which can have severe negative consequences in a violent encounter (he references Force Science's famous "Traffic Stop Study"). The implication for training then is to mind the pathways our training myelinates, and ensure we enforce good patterns. Movement – be it getting off the X or dropping your phone, is good.

Transitions

I wanted the head shot because that may be your reality, so having some introduction, some exposure to the concept of "the failure drill" is good – again, building confidence.

What's Not Here

All those "super-minimal" things like long distances (e.g. 25+ yards), deep movement, malfunctions, position changes, equipment transitions, cover/concealment, barriers, disability, lights, etc. All good things to know, but beyond minimum.

There are no reloads... on the clock. The data is strong in showing in-fight reloads in the private citizen self-defense context just don't happen (see: Active Self Protection's corpus of video data). It is an important skill, just not minimum. Note that with the 25 rounds of this test, the shooter will have to (re)load at least twice: once to start, once somewhere in the middle. At its most basic, the skill of (re)loading the gun must be exercised to perform the Assessment, and so the act of (re)loading won't be wholly novel. This is something I picked up from Claude Werner: the fundamentals of loading and unloading a gun. We take that action for granted because we've done it thousands of times, but there was a time you didn't know how to put cartridges into a magazine, you didn't know how to load your gun, you didn't know the proper order for unloading a semi-automatic handgun – you too had to learn these things. As such, just basic operation of the gun is part of minimum competency.

What's Hidden

Hidden in here are other minimum competency factors: safe gun handling, how to load a magazine, how to load and unload a gun, grip, stance, sight picture, sight alignment, recoil management, breathing, follow-through, reaction to stimulus (timer). They may not be called out by name in the choreography, but they are absolutely there and part of achieving minimum competency.

One-handed shooting

I'm still not sure if one-handed shooting is minimal or super-minimal. One-handed shooting is a skill to be taught, learned, and practiced. If I think back to my framing of "I have an afternoon to teach someone what they need to know", is that limited time well-spent by teach one-handed (in addition to two-handed and all the other things)? Maybe? I am undecided, but presently I think one-handed shooting is "one more thing", is scope creep, and it detracts from "the afternoon of teaching". I'd rather someone have a few things they can execute well, than a big toolbox they can barely utilize.

Karl raised the point that in many videos we see people shooting one-handed. True, but why are they shooting one-handed? Were they trained to do this? Or is it just some untrained response? I think that matters. And it could be argued if they just defaulted to one-handed, that perhaps the Assessment should have at least 1 one-handed string to introduce the concept. Ed Vinyard rightfully points out that if we don't measure/test things, it's easier to procrastinate training those things. So maybe there should be a one-handed string. I don't know yet.

Everything's a "shoot"

Not everything is a shoot, but everything in the Assessment is. I think it's important to train in the decision-making process, especially in terms of the shoot/no-shoot decision. Sometimes going for your gun is in response to shoot-decision, and this is basically the scenario we often drill: that the gun is holstered and only leaves the holster after the shoot decision is made (which is an argument for a rapid DTFAH). Sometimes the gun is already out but it's a no-shoot, which may turn into a shoot or may not. I think decision making is important, but I'm not sure if and how this can be quantified and reflected via the Assessment.

Administrative side-effects?

Some things in the Assessment are administrative, like rounding to 2.5 seconds at 5 and 7 yards, when the calculations came out to 2.3 for 5 and 2.7 for 7. I could justify saying that 2.5 is good for 7, with 5 being more complex since it adds in the side-step so it works out to have the same par time. But, do I have any risk of such things tainting the assessment? I was talking with Brian Hill about his Mixed 6. He admitted the reload string isn't quite in line with the rest of the drill, but it works "and Mixed 6 sounds cooler than Mixed 5". In my Rangemaster Master class, John Correia had us shoot his "10 Round Skill Check". I saw something in there (I forget exactly what) that didn't add up. John admitted it was a fudge to make the test work out. Three Seconds or Less does start variations to keep the 3 second par time across all strings. So, if administrative stuff is bad, I guess at least I'm in good company.

I want it to be as simple as possible, but no simpler. As Paul Howe says, "selection is a never-ending process", so...

Skill level, skill degradation

Is this the floor? Is this accurately placing the floor, the line of what defines minimum competence? I don't know... time will tell, I guess. One interesting element is skill degradation. It can and often does happen under stress. As Gabe White wrote on pistol-forum:

Still, when your skills tumble a thousand feet down the mountain, or however far they are going to fall depending on a person's 'coolness', because of stress and all the difficulty there might be when it's for real, don't you want to start at the top of the mountain rather than close to the bottom?

During the opening lecture of KR Training's Defensive Pistol Skills 1 class, we talk about "LTC vs. Reality". We call out a lesson from Paul Ford, former Austin PD SWAT. Paul was asked for one bit of advice to give someone about a gunfight and Paul said to expect to do about 70% of your worst day on the range. When you consider how far your skills may/will deteriorate, it begs setting the bar of competency high enough so any degradation of skill still leaves you operating with high skill.

More data, please

For sure, the Assessment could use more runs and data. I'd love to know how you do at shooting it. If you feel like going for extra credit, I'd love to know some data. Shoot it cold, as written. Send me your score, picture of your target, times for each string, what you shot it with, under what conditions, etc. As much data as you'd like to provide. Thank you.

I expect a v4 will come at some point...

Minimum Competency Assessment Checkpoints

Let's revisit the six checkpoints and see how it breaks down:

- Draw from concealment
  - The drill setup is to use your everyday carry gear, including your carry ammo if you can afford it. Yes, this implies carrying concealed (vs. open carry).

- - However, as I am changing my thinking to expand beyond the private citizen concealed carrier, it's really that first statement: using your EDC.
  - Every string starts from a draw.
    - No ready position starts, no table starts, etc.

- Getting multiple hits
  - There are strings of multiple shots, with a bias towards the "draw to first acceptable hit" (DTFAH) skill.

- In a small area
  - The body and head areas on the preferred KRT-2 target are representative of the small area to target.
    - Increased challenge (perhaps subsequent metric?) in targeting only the white-zones (body inner trapezoid, ocular)

- From close range
  - Heavy emphasis on <= 5 yard shooting.
  - Some work at 7 and 10 yards for confidence and practicalness (e.g. across a room)
    - Cold 10 yards to build confidence.

- Quickly
  - The par times are low enough, within statistical and data-reinforced thresholds.

- Using both hands
  - All strings are fired are two-handed.
  - There are different positional starts, because regardless of where our hands start, we want to get both of them on the gun.

And not much else. I am trying to keep it as focused and "on point" as possible.

I think this Assessment provides a fair attempt at realizing the skills relevant to minimum competency in defensive pistol skills to provide a means of assessing performance.

Final Thoughts

My hope for this work – the Assessment, but more so the reasoning underlying it – is that it makes a meaningful contribution towards the understanding of minimum competency. I go back to my origins: people passing the Texas LTC and thinking themselves good and done, when their targets look like they were peppered by a shotgun and they have no idea how to properly carry a gun. Is obtaining your Texas LTC an accomplishment? Yes! It's certainly a milestone along the road. And it's a far lot better than the Illinois CCL test (70% score, anywhere on a B-27 target with no time limits). The trouble with such tests is how people might weigh the test relative to their skills assessment; as Claude Werner points out, it can lead to poor outcomes:

> In the Not So Much successful incident, Calvin 'Mad Dog' Gonnigan shot at three people in Chicago who were celebrating Independence Day. A nearby Concealed Carry Licensee shot at 'Mad Dog' but only peripherally wounded him several times. 'Mad Dog' left but then came back to murder one of his victims by shooting her in the face and even further seriously wounding the other two victims. Eventually, the Police arrived from the District Headquarters, which was a block away, and took 'Mad Dog' into custody....

> Chicago, being an urban area, is unlikely to result in much practice. That's probably why 'Mad Dog' did most of his shooting at close range and probably why the CCL was not particularly successful. The Illinois qualification course can be passed by only hitting one shot out of 10 at 10 yards and that only has to hit an arm of the silhouette target.

We need to do better.

So what is sufficient? Is a sub-second draw necessary? Or do you just need to have a gun and the wherewithal to use it?

I want to reiterate an important point. This Assessment is intended to be a floor, not a ceiling. People want to know "Am I good enough?" Good enough for what? To be able to use a gun in self-defense. In order to make that assessment, we must be able to articulate what is involved both as a level to achieve and the means to get there.

I think it's unrealistic to have a never-ending "just get better" approach. Yes, I'm a firm believer in being better today than yesterday, but not everyone has the same outlook nor capabilities and capacity in life. Not everyone has the time, energy, and resources to get to a sub-second draw and drill out the X-ring at 25 yards. Do you need those skills to be able to successfully defend yourself? Are they the floor? I would say no. When Gabe White talks about his Performance Awards he says:

> ...these are difficult performance goals intended for use by enthusiasts who are going to devote a lot of effort, time, and resources to practicing and getting better... they are probably a lot more difficult technical level goals than you would address unless you were an enthusiast.... Again, these are goals, not standards, and they are intended for use by enthusiasts. There are lots and lots of people who have really gotten the job done in real life and they wouldn't reach any of these technical skill levels. They are very much intended for people who are self-motivated to do a lot of practicing and get as sharp as they can.

Chuck Haggard, from pistol-forum:

> I think people actually need, for the most part, far less technical shooting skill than we often think, not to say that people shouldn't train, it's just that most real world pistol fights just don't require that much marksmanship.

To understand what makes you minimally competent could influence what and how you prepare in the grander scheme. For example, perhaps you start your training with pistol proficiency, focusing on it until you achieve minimum competence. Then you put pistol skills into maintenance mode and start studying medical skills, or taking scenario/FoF training, or getting to the gym, or whatever. One can only focus on so much; to know when something is "good enough" and then you can switch to study something else? There's merit in that.

In his article "Skill Development – When are you good enough?", Greg Ellifritz wrote:

> *True mastery of any topic makes one a specialist. Becoming a specialist takes a long period of time. That time requirement is an opportunity cost that will most certainly reduce the time you have available to become adept at other survival skills.*

> *Beyond that, however, there are additional future consequences for attaining true mastery.*

> *What happens when you fail? No one can stay at the very top of their game forever. Challengers and upstarts are constantly clamoring for a shot at the title. Eventually, the "best" gets toppled. At that point, they are no longer "the best." Can your ego take that hit?*

> *What does it mean to make the mastery of a single topic your life's purpose when you realize that you are no longer making advancements in the field? At some point in your journey, you will reach a place where you can no longer make measurable improvement. When that happens, how will you feel?*

> *All of that potential pain and anguish is minimized if one seeks adept proficiency rather than absolute mastery.*

Greg references trainer Dan John about the 80/20 rule:

> *I like to throw myself passionately into a sport or activity until I reach about an 80 percent efficiency level. To go beyond that requires an obsession and degree of specialization that doesn't appeal to me. Once I reach that 80 percent level I like to go off and do something totally different.*

Greg brings up another facet: it's not just about going up the mountain, it's also about coming down. We won't stay young and fit forever. Maybe you can hit that sub-second draw in your 30s, but can you maintain that into your 60s? Maybe. What will it take to achieve that, and is it worth it? Is it even necessary? Because even in your 60s, you'll still want to know and have the confidence in knowing you can get the job done.

Not everyone is a hobbyist/enthusiast, but everyone has limitations: limited time, budget, and even desire/gumption. Yes, I think being better today than yesterday is a solid ethos, but not everyone thinks the same as I do. We don't all have the same goals, the same operating context, the same environment, the same constraints, the same resources, the same discipline, the same benefits and blessings, time, ability, motivation, or dedication. We are all on different and unique journeys. Nevertheless, we all possess the human right of self-defense, and with the right comes the responsibility to be "well regulated". To become as such is a road one must travel, and things such as this Assessment are but a milestone.

We want to grow our tent. In that outreach, we have to acknowledge the limits and constraints we all operate within. We have to work within those limits, giving a realistic and appropriate understanding of competency and sufficiency, yet balancing against attainability and the road and motivations to get there. It is important to bust false senses of ability – you need to KNOW what you can actually do. By knowing what it means to be minimally competent, you can have an appropriate and realistic understanding of your capabilities. Even if all you are is minimally competent, you are still competent.

We need to help people learn and grow. Crawl. Walk. Run. Crawling is learning gun parts, nomenclature, basic safety and marksmanship. Walking is getting people at least minimally competent. When people have competence that will build their confidence. I want to get people walking, and I want to help people walk through life with confidence.

Chapter 28
Our Top 10 Drills

In the Dec 24, 2017 episode of the Handgun World Podcast, John and I discussed 10 drills we think make a good baseline set of drills handgun shooters can use to maintain and develop skills. I calculated the relative difficulty of each drill using the process described earlier in this book.

Minimum Acceptable (25% of Grand Master)

The first three drills emphasize basic marksmanship and shooting at a moderate pace. Most state carry permit qualification courses of fire and beginner shooting program drills fit into this category, and all these drills require skill no better than 25% of GM to shoot perfect scores.

(1) NRA Basic Pistol Qualification

The 2017 version of the NRA Basic Pistol courses uses 4" circles. Shooters must put 5 shots into a 4" circle, at a minimum of 10 feet. Those able to pass the minimum level can repeat the drill at 15 feet (5 yards) and 20 feet (almost 7 yards). NRA Pistol instructors are required to be able to put 16 of 20 shots into a 6" circle at 15 yards. These drills have no time limit.

(2) Texas License To Carry (LTC) Test

The Texas LTC (formerly known as the Concealed Handgun License) shooting test has been in use since 1995, with well over 1 million shooters meeting this standard. It uses the B–27 target, counting the traditional 8, 9, 10 and X rings all as 5 points, with the 7 ring scored as 4, and anywhere inside the humanoid shape and outside the 7 ring counted as 3 points.

This adds the skills of bringing the gun from a ready position to the target quickly, and firing the required shots within a time limit, to the basic marksmanship tested by the NRA Basic Pistol qualification. As discussed earlier in the book, a perfect score on this test is 20–25% of GM level.

(3) The 5×5 drill

This drill, originally created by Gila Hayes of the Firearms Academy of Seattle, starts at the ready position. 5 shots into a 5″ circle, at 5 yards, in 5 seconds.

This drill is more challenging than the previous two. It requires shooting at a one–shot–per–second pace, similar to the fastest parts of the Texas LTC test, but at a much smaller target. (Based on what I've seen teaching the Texas LTC class for more than 20 years, Texas LTC holders who shot less than 90% on the state test would have a difficult time passing the 5×5 drill.)

As an additional challenge, Claude Werner suggests shooting this drill 5 times in a row, to ensure consistency and verify you didn't get lucky.

Reasonable Level (50% of Grand Master)

When I looked at the difficulty of many different law enforcement academy and police department qualification standards, most of them required being able to draw, reload and clear malfunctions, with speed and accuracy requirements in the 40–50% of GM level. We chose some widely used and well known drills and defined some par times roughly aligning with that difficulty level.

(4) Bill Drill

Draw and fire 6 shots, USPSA or IDPA target, 7 yards, 5 seconds (from concealment). All hits must be within the A-zone or 0-ring.

Bill gives a 3 second par time (from open carry) as a goal for a good shooter. In his book, *Practical Shooting*, Brian Enos uses a goal time of 2 seconds (from a competition holster) as a Master class benchmark. We chose a par time of 5 seconds, assuming a 2 second draw from concealment, and 0.5 second split times between shots.

(5) Minimum Competency Assessment

This 25 round drill adds the skills of drawing from concealment from different start positions, movement, two different target areas (head and body), at different distances. A passing score on this drill using the KRT-2 target is roughly 40% of GM.

(6) F.A.S.T.

The Fundamentals, Accuracy and Speed Test (F.A.S.T.) was created by Todd Green. It tests concealment draw, slide lock reload, and the ability to shoot at two different speeds – a slower speed to get two hits in the 3"x5" box, and the faster speed necessary to get 4 hits in the 8" circle. Typically the split times (shot to shot times) required in the 8" circle are twice as fast as those required for the 3"x5" box. Time penalties for missed shots in the 3"x5" box are twice as costly (2 seconds) as penalties for shots missing the 8" circle (1 second). Total score is raw time plus any penalties.

Todd considered runs under 5 seconds to be Master level. We chose a score of 10 seconds, from concealment, as our goal time for those training to the 50% level.

(7) Three Seconds or Less

The drill we use most often in our Defensive Pistol classes is the Three Seconds or Less drill. It's 9 strings, each 3 seconds long, requiring a variety of shooting skills on a KRT-2, USPSA, or IDPA target at 3 and 7 yards.

In addition to the skills tested by the Bill Drill and F.A.S.T., it adds one handed shooting, turning draws, and shooting while moving, in a series of 1, 2 and 3 shot strings.

A score of 90% or higher, working from concealment, requires roughly 50% of Grand Master skill if a 3 second par time is used. Faster par times can be used to increase the difficulty level.

More Challenging (70%+ GM, or IDPA Master)

These three drills are well known, widely used and very popular with high skill level shooters.

(8) "The Test"

"The Test" is shot using an NRA B-8 bullseye target. From the ready at 10 yards, shoot 10 rounds in 10 seconds freestyle. Scored by the rings, 90 points or better to pass. Made famous by Larry Vickers but often attributed to Ken Hackathorn.
There are many variations with more strings at different distances, working from the holster instead of ready, for those who want more challenge from this type of drill.

One popular variation is the **Super Test**, from Wayne Dobbs and Darryl Bolke
From the low ready
15 yards, 10 rounds, 15 seconds
10 yards, 10 rounds, 10 seconds
5 yards, 10 rounds, 5 seconds
For a total of 30 rounds, 300 points, 270 to pass.

(9) FBI qualification test (2000's version)

The 2000's versions of the FBI qualification test is also used in several national training programs. It has multiple strings at distances from 3 to 25 yards. It was first revised in 2013, and a new version of the course of fire was released in 2019.

(10) Standard IDPA 90 round classifier

In the Handgun World podcast and subsequent blog article, we listed Dot Torture (included in the next section) as drill #10. Dot Torture tests many skills, but has no time limit, and can be run at varying distances. Replacing Dot Torture in the list for the March 2019 printing of the book is the standard 90 round IDPA classifier.

The standard IDPA Classifier consisted of three stages testing many different skills. It's more complex to set up and run than the other drills on this list. Each string or stage of this test can be used as a standalone test. Duane Thomas' book *Mastering the IDPA Classifier* breaks down each

part and identifies goals for each stage, each string and each skill
necessary to shoot IDPA Master scores.

In Stage One:
Safely draw the pistol
Extend to fire
Transition between targets
Turning then drawing the pistol
Reloading the pistol
Executing precise shots
Shooting the pistol unsupported with either hand

Stage Two adds the following to the Stage One tasks:
Moving while shooting

Stage Three adds:
Shooting from cover
Moving from one shooting position to another

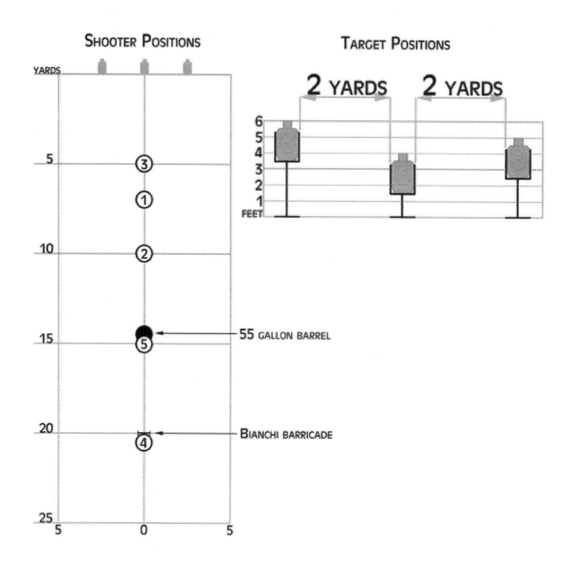

Stage 1 – 7 Yards			
String	Position	Instructions	Shots
1	1	Draw and fire two (2) shots to the body and one (1) to the head on T1.	3
2	1	Draw and fire two (2) shots to the body and one (1) to the head on T2.	3
3	1	Draw and fire two (2) shots to the body and one (1) to the head on T3.	3

4	1	Draw and fire two (2) shots at each head T1–T3.	6
*** Hits below the head area should be pasted before shooting String Five ***			
5	1	Start with gun in "WEAK" hand pointed down range at a 45° angle, safety may be off, but finger must be out of trigger guard, fire one (1) shot at each T1–T3. WEAK HAND ONLY	3
6	1	(Load 3 rounds MAX. in pistol) Start back to targets, turn and fire one (1) shot at each, T1–T3, reload from slide lock and fire one (1) shot at each, T1–T3	6
7	1	Draw and fire two (2) shots at each T1–T3 "STRONG" hand only.	6

Stage 2 – 10 Yards			
String	Position	Instructions	Shots
1	2	Draw and advance toward targets, fire 2 shots at each T1 – T3 while moving forward (all shots must be fired while moving) there is a forward fault line at the 5yd line for this string.	6
2	3	Draw and retreat from targets, fire 2 shots at each T1 – T3 while retreating (all shots must be fired while moving).	6
3	2	(Load 6 rounds MAX. in pistol) Start back to targets, turn and fire 2 shots at each T1 – T3, reload from slide lock and fire 2 shots at each T1 – T3.	12
4	2	Draw and fire 2 shots at each T1 – T3 "STRONG" hand only.	6

Stage 3 – 15/20 Yards			
String	Position	Instructions	Shots
1	4	Draw and fire 2 shots at each T1 – T3 from either side of the barricade, TACTICAL LOAD and fire 2 shots at each T1 – T3 from the opposite side of barricade.	12
2	4	Draw and fire 2 shots at each T1 – T3 from either	12

		side of the barricade, TACTICAL LOAD and advance to Position #5, fire 2 shots at each T1 – T3 from around either side of 55-gallon barrel.	
3	5	Draw, kneel, and fire 2 shots at each T1 – T3 from around either side of 55-gallon barrel.	6

Use a total match score (raw time and penalties) of 65 seconds as the 100% goal.

April 2019 update: After publication of the book, we developed a class called Top 10 Drills that runs students through the 10 drills in this section, using the par times and goals. The 90 round IDPA classifier is considerably more complex to set up and run than all the other drills in this section. Inspired by the Casino drill developed by Tom Givens, we developed a similar drill using the multi-shape KRT-1 target. This new drill only requires one target stand and one target, like all the others in the top 10.

The 16x16x16 drill (2023 update): 16 rounds at 16 feet within 16 seconds, onto a KRT-1 Target.

To set up, divide 16 rounds and one dummy round between two magazines. Use an unknown and varying round count between the two magazines. Load the gun with one of the magazines, and holster. Stand 16 feet from a KRT-1 target, gun concealed, hands relaxed at your side. Par time of 16 seconds equates to roughly 75% of USPSA GM 100% level (12 seconds). Many shooters find a 24 second par time (50%) to be a good initial goal for this drill.

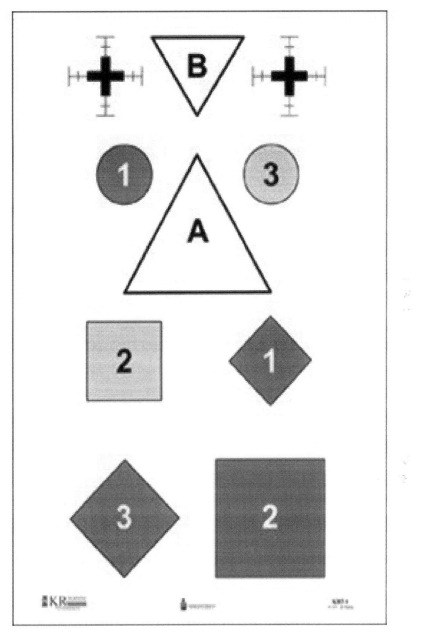

KRT-1 target available from letargets.com

On the signal, shoot each numbered shape on the target in any order. The shapes marked "1", shoot with 1 round. Those marked "2", shoot 2. Marked "3", shoot 3. Shoot 3 rounds in the A triangle and 1 in the B triangle. When you have a malfunction (dummy round), clear it (tap-rack) and continue. Whenever the gun runs empty, reload and continue until you've shot at all the shapes with the required number of rounds.

Your score is your time plus 1 second for every miss, and 1 second for any procedural (such as failing to shoot the right number of rounds for the drill, or right number of rounds on each shape). Total score under 16 seconds is roughly 60% of GM. Times below 12 seconds are roughly 83% of GM, with 10 seconds serving as the 100% standard.

In-the-moment decision making is a skill that's not tested by most formats of competition shooting. To do well on match day, typically what is required is the ability to quickly put together a stage plan, memorize it, and execute it without conscious thought in an automatic sequence. If all you want from this drill is to discover the fastest possible time you are capable of, you can plan out a sequence to minimize target transitions, and carefully load your mags so you can reload between two large shapes. But taking that route doesn't provide all the training you can get from the drill if you run it in a less structured way.

To get maximum value from this drill, randomize it. If you practice with a partner, have that person load your mags for you, so you don't know how many are in each one. Have your partner call a color or a shape or a number right before starting the timer. Then you have to shoot all the 2's, or all the triangles, or all the blue shapes first. Or they can give you a full sequence by calling these items in any order:

- 1,2,3, triangles (or) 1,2,3,A,B
- circle, square, diamond, triangle
- red, yellow, blue, triangles (A, B)

Each of those lists calls out all 8 shapes on the target using a sequence of 4 or 5 items. I think only giving the shooter one item to start, and tasking them with the job of figuring out how to finish, is harder — and a more realistic decision-making task.

No partner? Make a pile of 16 rounds and don't count when you load the two mags. Take some index cards, mark them with 1, 2, 3, circle, square, triangle, diamond, red, yellow, blue. Shuffle the deck. Draw a card and use the shape pair identified by what's on the card as your first pair to shoot.

Your times will be slower. Decisions take time. Reacting to the surprise of the gun locking open takes time. The drill, in a small way, can be used to build decision making speed, making choices between a few options in between sequences of 1-3 shots per target.

Readers familiar with the original version of the 16x16x16 drill will notice that we added a dummy round (and clearing a malfunction) to this drill, which adds another skill and increases the total time to run the drill for one second for high skilled shooters. We are keeping the 16 second goal time, as many high level shooters have run the drill in the 12-13 second range without the dummy round incorporated.

Chapter 29
Beyond the 10 Drills

This chapter includes many popular and widely used drills that may be of interest to those trying to progress beyond the 75% level.

Dot Torture

Dot Torture was developed by David Blinder and was modified and popularized by Todd Green. Like the NRA Basic Pistol test at the top of this test, it has no time limit and is purely a test of marksmanship. It uses small dots and requires two handed and one handed shooting, reloads, drawing, and other skills.

Dot Torture

© Todd Louis Green 2007, www.pistol-training.com
adapted from David Blinder, www.personaldefensetraining.com

1
5 shots slow fire

Date: _____
Score: _____ / 50
Distance: _____

2
draw, one shot (x5)

3 **4**
draw, 1 on 3, 1 on 4 (x4)

5
draw, five shots strong hand

6 **7**
draw, 2 on 6, 2 on 7 (x4)

8
ready, five shots weak hand

9 **10**
draw, 1 on 9, speed reload, 1 on 10 (x3)

Walkback Drill

The Walkback drill was documented on Todd Green's Pistol Forum site. The common theme is to work at maintaining constant accuracy (keeping 5 shots in a 3×5 card, for example), as you move backward. Some variations include a time limit – 3 shots in 3 seconds, working backward 1 yard at a time until you cannot keep all 3 shots on the card.

Four Aces

This simple drill, popularized by Ben Stoeger, is shot on a USPSA target at 7 yards. Draw, shoot 2, speed reload (no slide lock required), shoot 2.

The Wizard Drill

All strings have a 2.5 second par time. Use an IDPA target and shoot with your real world carry gear.

3 yd Draw and fire 1 head shot, strong-hand-only.
5 yd Draw and fire 1 head shot, both hands.
7 yd Draw and fire 1 head shot, both hands.
10 yd Draw and fire 2 body shots, both hands.

Scoring
Shots: 3 head, 2 body
Using an IDPA target, it is scored by the rings (-0, -1, -3).
You can drop 2 points and pass the drill.
Exceed any time limit – fail.
Miss a headshot – fail.

A simplified version of this drill, that we called the "**Wizard Jr.**" reduces the number of skills tested and increases the par time to 4.0 seconds.

3 yd Draw and fire 1 head shot, both hands.
5 yd Draw and fire 1 head shot, both hands.
7 yd Draw and fire 1 body shot, both hands.
10 yd Draw and fire 2 body shots, both hands.

This version is useful for those just learning the basics of how to draw.

STRATEGIES AND STANDARDS FOR DEFENSIVE HANDGUN TRAINING

Rangemaster Core Skills Test

The Rangemaster Core Skills test is similar to the FBI qualification course of fire. Multiple strings, multiple distances, many skills. It can be used as the basis for practice sessions, or to verify skills are maintained at an acceptable level. The test is 40 rounds, 200 points possible. IALEFI-QP target scored 5/3/0 OR RM-2 target scored 5/3, OR IDPA target, scored 5/3/1.

3 yards - Sidestep, draw, and fire 4 rounds
5 yards - Sidestep, draw and fire 4 to the chest, 1 to the head
5 yards - Start gun in dominant hand only, fire 4 rounds
5 yards - Start gun in non-dominant hand, fire 5 rounds
7 yards - Draw and fire 6 rounds
7 yards - Start at Ready, 3 rounds only in gun. Fire 3 rounds, reload, and fire 3 more rounds.
10 yards - Draw and fire 3 rounds.
15 yards - Draw and fire 4 rounds.
25 yards - Draw and fire 3 rounds.

Divide points by total time, multiply X 20 for Final Score.
Par Score = 100. 80-100 = Very good. 100-124= Advanced 125+= Master

5 Yard Roundup

Justin Dyal saw shooters well-grounded in the 7-15 yard range having problems in a closer, more time-pressured situation (e.g. taking too long, spraying and praying). He created this drill to address defensive shooting skills at close range. It is simple and easy to administer, requiring just an NRA B-8 repair center hung at 5 yards, and 10 rounds of ammunition. It should be shot from concealment (or duty gear). All strings have a par time of 2.5 seconds.
String 1 – from the holster, 1 shot, both hands
String 2 – from the ready, 4 shots, both hands
String 3 – from the ready, 3 shots, strong-hand-only
String 4 – from the ready, 2 shots, weak-hand-only

Score by the rings. 100 points maximum. > 90 is very good.

Eastridge Drill

Trainer Bryan Eastridge shared this drill, which was also selected as a Rangemaster Drill of the Month for December 2022. Par time for every string is 2.5 seconds for the advanced level. For those not yet at that level, determine the par time by working on the 15 yard string until it can be shot clean (all 0-ring) quickly, and use the fastest time for that run as the par time all strings. Bryan specified an IDPA target, but any target with an 8" circle in the chest and an ocular window in the head will work. Only hits in the 8" circle and the head circle count. Can be started from ready (easiest), open carry (medium), or concealed carry (harder). That allows one to make the drill progressively harder as your skills develop. When you can shoot it clean under the par time from The Ready, do it from the holster.

25 yards, 1 head shot
15 yards, 2 body shots
10 yards, 3 body shots
7 yards, 2 body, 1 head shot
5 yards, 3 body, 1 head shot
5 yards, strong hand only, 2 body shots
Total of 15 rounds. Score is number of hits in the -0 rings. Overtime shots do NOT count. Your goal is all 15 in the rings.

USPSA Classifiers

USPSA has a library of dozens of classifier stages available from their website. For each one, the 100% score can be identified using the classifier calculator on the USPSA website, or other classifier look up tools available online. The classifier stages, like the IDPA classifier, require multiple targets and other specialized props to set up and run correctly. In 2019, USPSA raised the high hit factors for many classifier stages in both USPSA and Steel Challenge formats, with some increasing as much as 5%.

Abbreviated IDPA Classifier

In 2017, the International Defensive Pistol Association responded to member feedback about issues administering the original IDPA Classifier.

In response, IDPA created a "5x5 Abbreviated" Classifier as an alternative means of classification. It requires a single IDPA target at 10 yards, 4 strings, and a total of 25 rounds fired. The course of fire, scoring, and grading can be found at idpa.com. In 2019, IDPA lowered the times for Master, Expert and the other ratings, making it approximately 5% harder to attain the IDPA Master rating.

Steel Challenge Stages

There are 8 official stages in the Steel Challenge pistol match. Each stage consists of 5 plates. Like the USPSA classifiers, there are published 100% scores shooters can use to compare their skills against that standard. The stages can be run on paper targets of the same size and shape as the steel targets. The stage descriptions can be found at SteelChallenge.com.

NRA Action Pistol Stages

There are 4 stages in the NRA Action Pistol format, also known as the Bianchi Cup. The paper targets used are the NRA D-1, often called the "tombstone" target. The Practical and Barricade events don't require a lot of props to run. Each part has a fixed par time, and scoring is based on points and X-ring hits. A perfect score is all X's, so calculating percentage for each stage is easy. More information can be found at https://competitions.nra.org/competitions/nra-national-matches/action-pistol-championship/.

The Practical Event: From the appropriate shooting line, the shooter fires at distances from 10 yards to 50 yards under varying time limits.

The Barricade Event: From within shooting boxes and behind barricades, a shooter fires at targets on either side of the barricade at different distances and under varying time limits.

The Falling Plate Event: From the appropriate shooting line, the shooter fires at 8 inch round steel plates arranged in banks of six at distances from 10 to 25 yards under varying time limits.

The Moving Target Event: From within shooting boxes at distances ranging from 10 to 25 yards, the shooter fires at a target moving from left to right with the target being exposed for only 6 seconds.

Competitors shoot from both standing and prone positions and are also required to shoot with both strong and weak hands at various stages.

Glock Shooting Sports Foundation stages

The Glock Shooting Sports Foundation matches use 3 main courses of fire. These are another national standard set of stages, shot by thousands of shooters over the past several decades. By looking at historical match results, it's easy to compare your scores to what the best competitors can do. The Glock stages can be found online at http://www.gssfonline.com/courses.cfm.

NRA National Pistol match courses of fire

These include traditional NRA bullseye events, such as the National Pistol Championship matches held at Camp Perry, OH, each year, and the Police Pistol Combat (PPC) matches. In both cases, scores for national-level champions can easily be found, making it possible to measure individual performance.

Federal Air Marshal Qualification

Prior to 9/11, this challenging course of fire was the pistol qualification standard for the Federal Air Marshal program. This was their definition of "minimum competency". Failing to meet the time standard for each string would result in an overall score of "fail", even if the combined scores and times for all strings met the overall standard. The skill level required to shoot the test with a perfect score is roughly 75% of GM, making this test one of the most difficult qualification standards used by any law enforcement agency, with difficulty increased by the per-string time requirements. Additionally, this course of fire is shot from concealment.

All targets set at 7 yards. QIT-99 target. Score 5 points inside the inner zones and 2 points anywhere in the bottle. Requires 135 / 150 to pass with no single stage time overage or re-shoot. This drill should be shot for score at the start of a practice session, with no warm-up or practice rounds fired before beginning the test.

Individual Drill	Starting Position	Time Allowed	Total Rounds	T1	T2	Total
1. Draw, one Round (twice)	Concealed	1.65 seconds (3.30 total)	2			
2. Double Tap (twice)	Ready	1.35 seconds (2.70 total)	4			
3. Rhythm fire 6 rounds at one target no more than 0.6 second between each shot	Ready	3.00 seconds	6			
4. One Shot, speed reload, one shot (twice)	Ready	3.25 seconds (6.50 total)	4			
5. One Round each at two targets three yards apart (twice)	Ready	1.65 seconds (3.30 total)	4			
6. 180° pivot, draw, one round each at three targets (twice) Turn left, then right.	Concealed	3.50 seconds (7.00 total)	6			
7. One Round, slide locks back; drop to one knee; reload; fire one round (twice)	Ready	4.00 seconds (8.00 total)	4			

Time: Cannot exceed total time for each drill. Example: Drill #1 - 1st time 1.70 seconds, 2nd time 1.55 seconds; Total = 3.25 seconds = Go.
Must achieve a "GO" on each drill.

The Casino Drill

This drill, developed by Tom Givens, uses the DT-2A target. Start with 7 rounds in your holstered pistol, with two additional 7 round magazines in magazine pouches on your belt. On the buzzer, shoot the "1" shape with 1 round, the "2" shape with 2 rounds, "3" shape with 3 rounds, and so on, for a total of 21 rounds fired. Reload each time the gun goes to slide lock, which will occur on the 1st shot on the "4" and after the 4th shot on the "5". It's shot at 5 yards, with a par time of 21 seconds, so you are shooting 21 rounds, in 21 seconds, at 15 feet.

Shots outside the shapes or procedural errors (wrong number of rounds per shape, reload at wrong time, etc.) are one second each. A total time (clean) of 15 seconds is 75–80% skill, with 12 seconds considered a "100%" time. As with other drills, there have been scores shot that are faster than 12 seconds. 100% is not the absolute limit of human performance.

The drill tests presentation from the holster, rapid, multiple shots on multiple targets, empty gun reload, and the mental task of being able to keep up with where you are in the process during the entire drill. Passing is defined as completing the test with a total score (par time plus errors) of less than 21 seconds. A more restrictive score is to consider the test a "fail" unless all shots are hits and all procedures are followed.

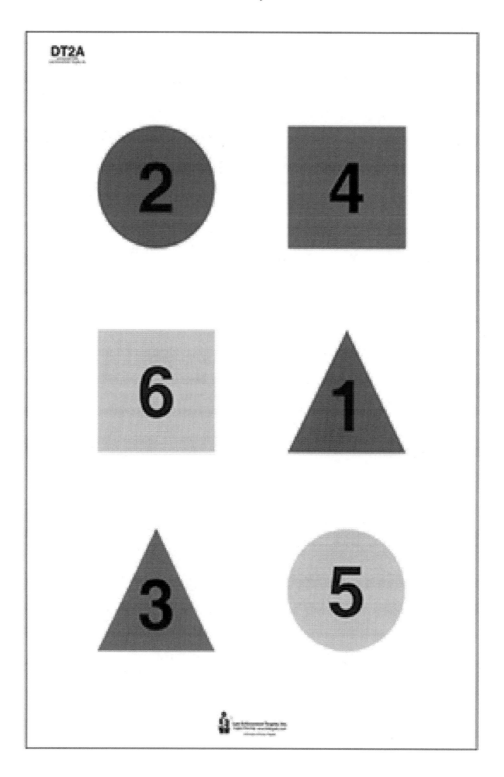

FBI Bullseye

This course is shot two handed on the FBI-IP1 target. 10-8 Consulting also created a PDF that can be printed on 8.5"x11" paper that has the correct dimensions for this course of fire. The 10-ring is approximately 3.5", with 9 and 10 rings black, plus 7 and 8 rings. Hits outside the 7 are misses.

1) 25 yards, 10 rounds, 4 minutes

all remaining shots at 15 yards
 2) 5 shots in 15 seconds
 3) 5 shots in 15 seconds
 4) 5 shots in 10 seconds
 5) 5 shots in 10 seconds

30 rounds, 300 possible,
260 to pass.

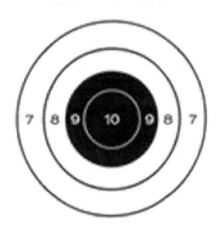

The estimated difficulty level of this course of fire is that a perfect score of 300 is roughly 75-80% of GM. This course of fire is used in FBI instructor training and in many schools and training programs.

Gabe White Technical Skills Tests

All are shot on a single USPSA Metric or IDPA target or similar, with either a 4" circle or 3×5" card added to the head, at a distance of 7 yards. The shooter can start with hands at sides, hands at high torso, or a hands-up surrender position. At the start signal, the shooter draws and engages the target exactly as required by the drill. No extra shots are allowed. Your score is your time, with penalties added for shots outside the A/-0 zone. B/C/-1 zone hits add .25 seconds per shot. D-zone hits add 1 second per shot. Misses add 2 seconds per shot. Head shots that land in the body count as misses. Body shots that land in the head count as lucky shots and are scored.

The Bill Drill (six shots to the body)
Failure to Stop (two shots to the body and one shot to the head)
Immediate Incapacitation (two shots to the head)
The Split Bill Drill (four shots to the body and two to the head)

Bakersfield Qualification

This course of fire was developed by Mike Waidelich of the Bakersfield, CA police department in the 1980's

All of this begins from the holster at each distance, if you think the times are generous from the low ready.

    2 rounds in 1.5 seconds at 10 feet
    ("No one should be closer than that.")
- 2 rounds in 2.0 seconds at 20 feet
   ("The length of a car.")
- 2 reload 2 in 6.0 seconds (8.0 for revolvers) at 30 feet
    ("From the curb to the front door.")
- 2 rounds in 3.5 seconds at 60 feet
    ("From the opposite curb to the front door.")

The 10-point scoring zone on the silhouette target was, as best Mike could recall, a 7-inch circle, with the next zone (9 points) measuring 9×13 inches. A hit anywhere else on the silhouette scored 6 points.

(Note: the grey and black scoring areas on the KRT-2 are very close to these measurements, making it an excellent target to use to shoot this particular drill, if pasted onto a USPSA or IDPA cardboard backer.)

Time penalties are set as follows:

"The time was flexible in that there were penalties for overtime. The penalties were 1 point per quarter second over the time allowed for the string. So, if you fired 2 in 1.5 seconds at 10 feet, you got zero penalties. At 1.75 seconds you lost 1 point. At 2.0 you lost 2 points, etc. "

Passing score– 80 with 100 points possible.

DR Performance Practice Deck

The DR Performance Practice Deck is available as an IOS app and a physical deck of cards, with content developed by Dave Re and the digital version implemented by John Daub & Hsoi Enterprises. In both formats, the Practice Deck provides 52 different drills that shooters can use to practice a wide variety of skills and drills. Most of the drills can be set up with a few props and target stands. Goal times for the drills in the deck can be calculated by using the individual skill component values provided earlier in this book.

Drill Analysis

In 2022 I compiled data from my Advanced Handgun road course to expand John Hearne's automaticity chart to include more drills, such as The Test, the 5 Yard Roundup, The Wizard, Four Aces and a 15 yard Bill Drill. That data mapped to John's chart like this:

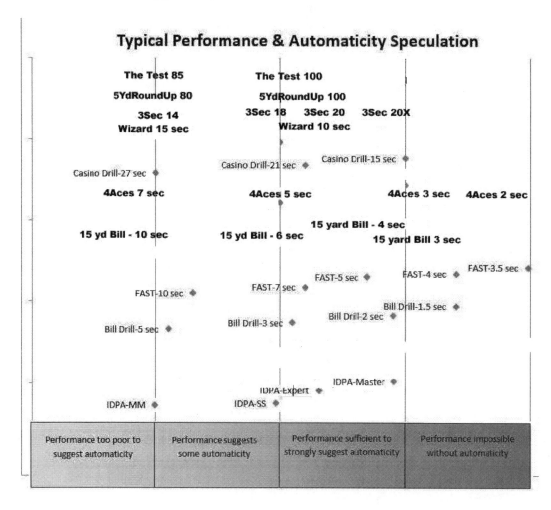

If you use the Hearne chart and set a life goal of keeping your skills inside the "performance sufficient to strongly suggest automaticity", these drill goals make a good set of standards to aspire to or maintain.

The Test – 90 points
5 Yard Round Up – 90 points
Three Seconds or Less – 18 points
Wizard Drill – clean, no overtime shots
Casino Drill – 21 seconds no penalties
Four Aces – 5 seconds all A's
15 yard Bill Drill – 6 seconds all A's
F.A.S.T. – 7 seconds
7 yard Bill Drill – 3 seconds all A's
El Presidente – 10 seconds all A's
FBI Bullseye – 250 points
Failure Drill – 2.5 seconds all A's
Split Bill Drill – 4.0 seconds all A's
Immediate Incapacitation – 2.5 seconds (4" circle for head)
Bakersfield PD Qualification – 80 points

Essentially the goal is IDPA Expert or the boundary between USPSA B and C class.

Chapter 30
Top 10 Drills for Skill Development

Since the publication of the first edition of this book, we have been using our original list of Top 10 drills integrated into our existing curriculum, in private lessons, and in a dedicated Top 10 Drills course where each drill is shot in order for score.

Influenced by the list of skills defined for Minimum Competency, we revisited the Top 10 Drills list, this time focusing on the skills tested by each drill, rather than the difficulty of the drill relative to the GM standard. The difficulty of any drill can be adjusted by changing par times. Our list of skills is here:

1) Accuracy
2) Present from Ready (Ready)
3) Draw from holster (Draw)
4) Targets at Multiple Distances (MultiYard)
5) Different sized target areas, same distance (HeadBody)
6) Movement
7) Reload
8) Strong Hand Only (SHO)
9) Weak Hand Only (WHO)
10) Multiple Targets Per String (MultiTarget)
11) Use of Cover
12) Thinking

"Thinking" occurs when the process of the drill cannot be memorized. With a training partner, this can be accomplished using a Casino or KRT-1 target that has different shapes, colors and numbers. The partner can call out a shape, color or number for the shooter to engage. John Murphy of FPF Training and John Hearne of Two Pillars Training, among others, use colored lasers or LED lights to indicate targets as shoot or no-shoot, sometimes changing the target mid-drill to teach in-fight decision making. For solo practice, loading magazines with random numbers of rounds, inserting dummy rounds, and changing the drill sequence can inject mid-drill decision making.
No single drill, even the more complex ones, addressed all 12 skills.

For the revised top 10 list, we considered all of these drills:

DRILL	ROUNDS	SKILLS
NRA	20	1
5x5	25	2
Bill Drill	6	2
The Test	10	2
Super Test	30	3
LTC	50	3
Four Aces	4	3
Wizard Jr.	10	4
Bakersfield Qual	10	4
El Presidente (6 seconds)	12	4
Min Comp Assessment	25	5
FAST (10 sec)	6	5
Wizard	10	5
Five Yard Roundup	10	5
Eastridge Drill	15	6
FBI	50	6
Dot Torture	60	6
Casino Drill	21	6
16x16x16 (2023)	16	7
3M	9	7
Three Seconds or Less	20	9
FAM qual	30	9
RM Core Skills	40	9
IDPA 90	90	10

After a lot of discussion, we pared the list down to these 10:

#	DRILL	SKILLS
1	NRA	Accuracy
2	5x5	Accuracy, Ready
3	Super Test (2x time)	Accuracy, Ready, MultiYard
4	Wizard Jr. (4 sec)	Accuracy, Draw, MultiYard, HeadBody
5	Min Comp Assessment	Accuracy, Draw, MultiYard, HeadBody, Movement
6	FAST (10 sec)	Accuracy, Draw, MultiYard, HeadBody, Reload
7	16x16x16 (24 sec)	Accuracy, Draw, MultiYard, HeadBody, Reload, Malfunction, Thinking
8	Three Seconds or Less	Accuracy, Ready, Draw, MultiYard, HeadBody, Reload, SHO, WHO
9	RM Core Skills	Accuracy, Ready, Draw, MultiYard, HeadBody, Reload, SHO, WHO
10	IDPA 90 (Expert level)	Accuracy, Ready, Draw, MultiYard, HeadBody, Reload, SHO, WHO, MultiTarget, Use of Cover

This sequence of drills, with adjusted par times, may be a better self-guided training program than our original list. In general, the best way to use these drills is to start with drill #1, run it with no par time until it can be shot clean, then add our recommended starting par time. Work on that until you can shoot the drill clean at that par time before moving onto the next drill.

For the 5x5 drill, start with a 10 second par time and speed up until you can do it in 5 seconds, 5 times in a row, clean, before proceeding to the next drill on the list.

For the Super Test, double all the par times:

5 yards, 10 shots, 10 seconds
10 yards, 10 shots, 20 seconds
15 yards, 10 shots, 30 seconds

Those are the level 3 goals to meet before moving forward to drill #4.

For the fourth drill, use the "junior" version of the Wizard drill, with a 4 second par time. You should revisit the Super Test and Wizard Drill later in your development with the original version and par times.

Use a 10 second par time for your first attempts at the F.A.S.T. drill. After you have passed drills 8 and 9, revisit the F.A.S.T. and work toward a 7 second par time goal.

Use a 24 second par time for your initial attempts on the 16x16x16 drill.

If you can shoot the IDPA 90 round classifier at the Expert level, consider that a "graduation" from the Top 10 Skill Development ladder. From this point, you'll need a list of maintenance drills for practice and evaluation.

Chapter 31
Maintenance and Evaluation Drills

In a perfect world, every armed citizen will have the time, money, and range access to develop their skills to the automaticity level, and maintain those skills through frequent dry fire and occasional live fire practice sessions. For those previously motivated to only meet the state minimum, we encourage you to put in the work to pass our Minimum Competency standards. That gives you reasonably acceptable proficiency in the 5 most important skills. Any of the first 5 drills in our Top 10 Skill Development list are suitable for practice and evaluation.

For those willing to put in the extra effort to reach the Automaticity level, here's a set of drills that covers 11 of the 12 skills in 100 rounds.

Start with an IDPA target

Failure Drill – 2 body, 1 head, from 7 yards, drawing from concealment, USPSA or IDPA target. 2.5 second par time, all A's.

Eastridge Drill –This 15 round drill is great for understanding the relationship between target difficulty and shooting speed, and tests 6 core skills. Shoot it clean drawing from concealment, using a 3 second par time for each string.

Rangemaster Core Skills – this 40 round course of fire covers 9 of the 12 skills, missing only Malfunction, Use of Cover, and Thinking.

Repair your IDPA backer with a F.A.S.T. target, or use the 8" circle and paste a 3x5 index card on the head.

F.A.S.T. – This 6 round drill is very well designed, evaluating accuracy from the draw, cadence (split times between head and body shots), first shot after a reload, and the reload itself. 7 seconds or less par time.

Paste a B8 target over the 8" circle

The Test – 10 rounds, 10 shots, 10 yards into a B-8 bullseye, goal is 90 points or better.

Tape or replace your B8 target.

Five Yard Round-Up – This 10 round drill is great for teaching you cadence related to two handed, strong hand only and weak hand only shooting.

Paste a KRT-1 target over your IDPA target

16x16x16 (2023 version) – this 16 +1 dummy round drill adds Malfunction and Thinking, so this drill plus the RM Core Skills gives you 11 of the 12 skills. Goal of 20 seconds or less.

You can practice "use of Cover" doing dry fire work at home, using furniture and doorways. If you have access to a range that has barricades, incorporating a barricade into one or more strings of the Rangemaster Core Skills test will check that remaining skills box.

Chapter 32
Closing Thoughts

In our ongoing research into the history of defensive handgun technique and training, we've read hundreds of books and articles, watched many hundreds of hours of digitized film and video spanning the past century, and learned as much as we could from many accomplished, experienced, and thoughtful people. The goal of this book was to provide our perspective on the topics we've covered, and perhaps add some new thoughts and analysis to that existing body of work. The intention was to provide information of interest to the 1%: instructors, competition shooters, serious shooters motivated to train beyond state minimums, and anyone involved in firearms training.

If you were part of the 99% when you started reading, and we've inspired you to work your way through the 10 drills, try any of the other courses of fire discussed in the book, attend a training course, shoot a match, or just pick up your gun and practice some dry fire shots and dry fire draws, welcome to the 1%. If you were already part of the 1%, we hope the final section of this book will help you identify drills and analyze your performance as you progress. If you train others at any level, from full time professional to weekend coach to informal advisor to friends and family, the information should be useful to you in choosing drills and goals for your students.

We welcome your feedback, questions, comments and corrections. We can be reached at rehn@krtraining.com, www.krtraining.com, blog.krtraining.com, hsoi@hsoi.com, and blog.hsoi.com. We, Karl and John, can be found teaching classes at the KR Training A-Zone facility in Central Texas, presenting at the occasional conference, and at any facility that wants to host one or both of us for a class at your location.

APPENDIX 1
RED DOT SIGHTS:
BEYOND THE ONE PERCENT

Red dot sights have been used on pistols since the late 1980's. Bullseye shooters were early adopters, followed by USPSA shooters in the early 1990's. The red dot sights in use during those years were mounted to the frame of the pistol, and the sight itself was a tube with front and rear lenses, similar to traditional rifle and handgun hunting scopes. Several vendors introduced single lens, open designs in the 1990's, and this type of sight became standard on USPSA Open division guns by the end of the decade. A few gunsmiths, notably David Bowie of Bowie Tactical Concepts, began mounting the smallest of the red dot sights on pistol slides.

Over the past decade, improvements in small red dot sights caused renewed interest in slide-mounted red dots. Multiple vendors now produce ruggedized sights intended for slide-mounted use, including models narrow enough to fit on single-stack compact carry pistols. Many gun makers are now offering factory models with slides configured to accept a red dot sight, and some complete guns with red dot sights installed. Most of the models include tall backup iron sights, visible through the red dot sight, but some factory models have no iron sights at all, only the slide mounted dot.

After 20 years of red dot sights being used by the one percent: competition shooters, students in classes beyond state minimums and industry product reviewers, the slide mounted red dot sight is now being adopted by some of the 99% that do not practice or train. This change is good for those in the business of selling and gunsmithing pistols, red dot sights, and holsters. It's particularly good for those trainers who have established themselves as subject matter experts in red dot pistol shooting skills.

Most advocates for slide mounted red dot sights insist that tall backup iron sights are necessary, both to be used in the event the red dot sight fails and no dot is visible, and to aid the new red dot sight user in finding the dot when the gun is brought from the holster or ready position to the target. When a shooter using iron sights brings the gun up to the eye-target line, there are multiple visual cues used to align the pistol. The slide itself, the view of the sights looking over them as the gun is raised, and finally the relative alignment of front and rear. The iron-sight presentation is one of using a wide range of visual information to make adjustments to the gun's movement to end with an acceptable sight picture aligned with the intended target. The process is different for the red dot sight. Often, the unskilled user will bring the gun up, see target through the sight's window, but no dot. When this occurs, the only visual information available to the shooter is the (mis)alignment of the backup irons. The unskilled user rarely uses the irons and instead wiggles the gun around up/down/left/right hoping to pick up the dot within the window. This takes time.

In 2015-2016, supported by funding by the Texas A&M Huffines Institute, Dr. Penny Riggs, Karl Rehn, and Blaise Collins tested 118 shooters' ability to use iron sights, lasers, and red dot sights with and without backup iron sights. The results of that test have been presented at conferences, on podcasts and on the KR Training official blog (blog.krtraining.com). Additional analysis was completed by Martin Nau in 2018-2019, with scientific paper in preparation for submission as a journal article.

In our study, most of the participants, regardless of skill level, had limited experience with pistols with red dot sights. The testing focused on ability to get an accurate first shot hit at 5 and 10 yards within 1.5 seconds, starting at a ready position. The table below shows the relationship between ability to get an acceptable hit (inside the IDPA target zero-ring) within the 1.5 second time limit, as a percentage of the percentage of the 118 shooters we tested that were able to do it.

	Novice	Carry Permit	Post-Carry	Instructor
Iron Sights	81.6%	94.2%	98.3%	99.2%
Laser Only	72.6%	93.4%	97.8%	93.4%
Red Dot/Irons	67.0%	82.8%	86.4%	95.5%
Red Dot Only	63.2%	71.0%	83.3%	86.4%

Table A1: Performance vs. Skill Level

The most common problem was inability to find the dot in the window before the time was up. Presentation of the gun to target, under time pressure, from the ready or the holster, is a part of most post-carry-permit level training. It is not part of the practice regimen of the typical carry permit holder, who is unlikely to own a shooting timer, do any dry fire practice, or shoot any timed drills in live fire. Incorporation of backup irons, particularly for those with some shooting experience (the "Carry Permit" column), makes a significant difference in performance – more than 10%. Having the iron sights available when the dot was not visible was of less value to the novices in our study, as they lacked the experience to revert to a traditional sight picture when the dot was not available.

The marketing message about red dot sights is that they make shooting easier. Some red dot advocates explain that the red dot sight allows target focus, in a single focal plane, which matches what our vision does under stress. Many high skill level shooters report that the ability to shoot more precisely, particularly at longer distances, is easier using a red dot than iron sights. And older shooters, dealing with loss of ability to shift visual focus and focus at closer distances, find the red dot sight easier to use than traditional irons. For the one percent who are willing to put in the work and develop the ability to find the dot quickly as the gun comes to the eye-target line, the red dot has many advantages. But our data (and experiences on the range working with the growing number of students bringing red dot-equipped guns to classes) indicates that the slide mounted red dot sight may not produce better results for those un-motivated to put in the effort necessary to have a reliable draw or gun index.

The most common situation is a carry permit level shooter who removes the rear sight from his pistol, replacing it with a red dot sight, thinking that the front sight alone will serve as sufficient "backup irons". Worse, that person, confident in his ability to run the dot, having done no dry work and no live fire practice beyond zeroing the dot at close range, will begin carrying that configuration. That approach is a recipe for disaster. There are rear sight mounts that provide backup irons available for those wanting a low cost way to install a red dot, but the best approach is to have the slide milled to mount the sight lower, or purchase a factory model that has the mount integral to the slide.

Several times in the past year, we have had students show up to post-carry-permit level classes with red-dot sight equipped guns who had not done the necessary homework, assuming that either class would provide them that opportunity, or that their slow fire target shooting practice indicated finding the dot when drawing at speed would not be a problem. In a few cases, the guns did not have back up irons. In most cases, those students struggled, compared to others with similar skill levels on the line using iron sights, and were not able to make par times for drills because of time spent "dot hunting".

The reality of group classes is that instructors have allocated specific blocks of time to cover different topics in the curriculum, and when a few students fall behind, it's unfair to the others in the class to allocate additional time to remedial work, often at the cost of cutting other material at the end of the class due to time constraints. Our standard solution, which many trainers do not have available, is to move the struggling student(s) off the line and send them to a separate shooting area to get additional instruction from one of the class assistants, either spending the remaining time in class with the assistant or (if they improve enough) rejoining the main group.

Study results indicated that the visible laser, at least at close distances, had a shorter learning curve and produced results equal to iron sights, particularly for novice shooters. Lasers, unlike red dot sights, allow the user to aim the gun without bringing the gun to the eye-target line, with pure target focus. For lower skilled shooters looking for a short-learning curve alternative to iron sights for shots at the most likely defensive pistol shot distances, visible lasers may be a viable alternative.

With the growth in sales of, and interest in, red dot sights on pistols, it's likely that instructors of carry permit classes are going to have students struggling with "dot hunting" in their classes, as will instructors teaching entry level defensive pistol courses. If you are an instructor and you don't currently have any experience running a slide mounted red dot pistol, getting that experience should be a priority. Coaching yourself through that work to learn to run a red dot will be essential in developing the skills to assist students. Several of the red dot specific trainers have instructor certification courses. These may have value to you in improving your ability to coach others, but instructors considering attending those classes should first take a student level class in red dot pistol shooting. Otherwise you risk being the instructor-class equivalent of the new red dot pistol owner that shows up for a defensive pistol course.

Should you put a red dot pistol on your daily carry gun? Our standard response to that question should be no surprise to readers: baseline your existing skills using the drills covered in this book. Then, if possible, leave your existing carry gun alone, and set up a second gun with a red dot sight. Practice with that gun until your skill with it matches or exceeds your iron sighted baseline. That practice should include low light shooting and one handed shooting. Pay close attention to the number of times you lose time on presentation when the dot is not visible. Lifesaving skills have to be consistent. Ten times out of 10 with no failures. If you are shooting GM scores 80% of the time, and lose a full second on the draw searching for the dot the other 20%, are those odds acceptable? Consistency, not "single best run", is the right way to measure critical skills. Is 70% of your worst practice run good enough? If you put in the work, consistency and skill can be achieved. Without the work, the potential for disaster and failure to get an acceptable first shot hit increases.

REFERENCES

The majority of the material referenced in this book can be found online. Some items have restricted distribution, limited to members, paying users or journal subscribers.

ONLINE ARTICLES
"A Separate Thread for Anatomical Correctness of Targets", https://pistol-forum.com/showthread.php?9306-A-Separate-Thread-For-Anatomical-Correctness-Of-Targets, 2013.

Butler, Chris. "Firearms Training for Real World Assaults," https://www.forcescience.com/2022/02/firearms-training-for-real-world-assaults/, 2022.

Danger Close Group. "Influential Gun Industry Influencers," 2018.

Ellifritz, Greg. "Ken Hackathorn's Wizard Drill", https://www.activeresponsetraining.net/ken-hackathorns- wizard-drill, 2015.

Ellifritz, Greg. "Requiem for an Unsung Hero," https://www.activeresponsetraining.net/requiem-for-an-unsung-hero, 2021.

Ellifritz, Greg. "Skill Development – When Are you Good Enough?" http://www.activeresponsetraining.net/skill-development-when-are-you-good-enough, 2015.

"Handgun Standards 1", Handgunlaw.us, 2019.

Harris, Mary and Miller, Kari. "Gender and perceptions of Danger", Sex Roles, 2000.

Hopson, John. "Behavioral Game Design", www.GamaSutra.com, 2001.

House, Sherman. "The Tennessee Handgun Carry Permit Class", www.CivilianDefender.com, 6 April 2016.

Houston Chronicle staff. "4,000 guns stolen from Houston cars over past year, authorities say", Houston Chronicle, https://www.chron.com/news/houston-texas/article/Guns-stolen-Houston-cars-17478178.php, 20 Sep 2022.

"Input on Current Project" thread, https://pistol-forum.com/showthread.php?11067-Input-on-Current-Project, 2014.

Lambert, Craig. "Spaced Education Boosts Learning", www.HarvardMagazine.com, 11 September 2009.

"Lessons from Mt. Stupid", https://xonitek.com/lessons-from-mt-stupid/, 2014.

"Red Dot Study – Key Points", blog.krtraining.com, 2017.

"The Bell-Curve: Shooting Practice by the Odds", Growing Up Guns blog, 2017.

Transportation Security Agency (TSA). "Firearms Discovered at TSA Checkpoints", USA Today, https://www.usatoday.com/story/travel/flights/2016/01/27/tsa-guns-weapons/79362942/, 27 Jan 2016.

Werner, Claude. "Defense of Others," https://thetacticalprofessor.net/2021/10/09/defense-of-others/, 2021.

Werner, Claude. "List of Negative Outcomes," 2014.

Werner, Claude. "Practice Priorities for the Armed Citizen," www.TacticalProfessor.com, 2014.

Werner, Claude. "The Importance of the First Shot, https://thetacticalprofessor.net/2021/04/09/the-importance-of-the-first-shot/, 2021.

Werner, Claude. "Why I hate the -3 zone",
https://thetacticalprofessor.net/2014/08/10/why-i-hate-the- 3-zone/,
2014.

White, Gabe. "Technical Skills Tests,"
http://www.gabewhitetraining.com/technical-skills-tests/, 2022.

BOOKS

Ayoob, Massad and Hearne, John. "Inside the Defender's
    Head" from Straight Talk on Armed Defense, 2016.

Enos, Brian. Practical Shooting: Beyond Fundamentals, 1991.

Hayes, Gila. Effective Defense: the Woman, the Plan, the Gun,
1994.

National Rifle Association. NRA CCW course materials, 2019.

Seeklander, Michael. Your Defensive Pistol Program, 2017.

Stoeger, Ben. Skills and Drills, 2017.

Stoeger, Ben. Dry Fire Reloaded, 2017.

Suarez, Gabe. Red Dot Combat Pistols II, 2016.

Texas Engineering Extension Service. Critical Asset Risk
    Management (MGT-315), 2017.

Thomas, Duane. Mastering the IDPA Classifier, 2014.

PERSONAL COMMUNICATION
Collins, Blaise, Nau, Martin, Rehn, Karl, and Riggs, Penny.
Red Dot Study (interim report), 2018.

Dozier, Bill. Analysis of KR Training student data, 2017.

Hearne, John. "Who Wins, Who Loses, and Why: Understanding Human Performance When Death is on the Line," Presentation, 2022.

Jewell, Robert. Email, 2019.

Sandoval, Robyn. A Girl and a Gun club national HQ, A Girl and A Gun, 2017.

JOURNAL ARTICLES
Bray, Molly S.; Dishman, Rod; and Jackson, Andrew S. "Self-regulation of Exercise Behavior in TIGER study," Society of Behavioral Medicine, 2013.

Burson, Katherine. "Consumer-product Skill Matching: The effects of difficulty on relative self-assessment and choice," Journal of Consumer Research, 2007.

Dishman, Rod. "Problem of Exercise Adherence: Fighting Sloth", National Association for Physical Education in Higher Education, 2001.

Dishman, Rod. "Self-Motivation and Adherence to Theraputic Exercise", Journal of Behavioral Medicine, 1981.

Gallinat, Jurgen; Gleich, Tobias; Kuhn, Simone; and Lorenz, Robert C. "Video game training and the reward system," Frontiers in Human Neuroscience, Feb 2015.

Gerbering, Julie L., MD, MPH; Marks, James S., MD, MPH; Mokdad, Ali H. Mokdad, PhD,; and Stroup, Donna F., PhD, MSc. "Actual Causes of Death in the United States, 2000," Journal of American Medical Association, Vol 291, No. 10. March 10, 2004.

Glass, Arnold L.; Shors, Tracey J.; and Sisti, Helene M. "Neurogenesis and the Spacing Effect: Learning and Memory," 2007.

Ivory, Sebastian L.; Yamane, David; and Yamane, Paul. "The Rise of Self-Defense in Gun Advertising: The American Rifleman, 1918-2017," Paper prepared for session on "Guns and Markets" University of Arizona Gun Studies Symposium, 20 October 2017.

Kravitz, Len. "Exercise Motivation: What Starts and Keeps People Exercising?" 2008.

Lott, John, "Concealed Carry Permit Holders Across the US," Crime Prevention Research Center, 2012.

Meyer, Glenn. "Evaluation of Women's Self Defense and Weapons Related Aggressive Priming," 2014.

Shapira, Harel, and Simon, Samantha J. "Learning to Need a Gun". Quantitative Sociology, March 2018.

REPORTS
2013 LTC reports, Texas Department of Public Safety, 2013.

2014 LTC reports, Texas Department of Public Safety, 2014.

2015 LTC reports, Texas Department of Public Safety, 2015.

1991 Exercise Adherence Digest, Education Resources Information Center, 1991.

ActionFan and the Path to Participation in Shooting Sports, NSSF, 2017.

American Time Use Survey, Bureau of Labor Statistics, 2015.
Analysis of Sport Shooting Participation 2008-2012, NSSF, 2013.
Consumer Sentiment Study, National Shooting Sports Foundation, 2017.

Economic Impact of Target Shooting, National Shooting Sports Foundation, 2013.

Firearm Justifiable Homicides and Non-Fatal Self Defense Gun Use, Violence Policy Center, June 2015.

Miniaturized Red Dot Systems for Duty Handgun Use – Aaron Cowan, Sage Dynamics, 2017.

Needs-Based Consumer Segmentation Report, National Shooting
Sports Foundation, 2014.

NSGA Shooting Sports Participation, National Shooting Sports
Foundation, 2016.

Profile of IDPA Shooters, National Shooting Sports Foundation,
2014.

Scholastic Shooting Sports Industry Intelligence Report, NSSF,
2016.

Sport Shooting Participation in the US in 2014, National Shooting
Sports Foundation, 2014.

Understanding Activities that Compete with Hunting and Target
Shooting, NSSF, 2011.

Women Gun Owners, 2014 edition, National Shooting Sports
Foundation, 2014.

WEBSITES
www.Tacticalprofessor.com, Claude Werner

www.idpa.com, International Defensive Pistol Association

www.nra.org, National Rifle Association

tpwd.texas.gov, Texas Parks and Wildlife

www.census.gov, United States Census Bureau

www.uspsa.org, United States Practical Shooting Association

TotalProtectionInteractive.com forum

Pistol-forum.com forum

www.krtraining.com KR Training

Blog.krtraining.com KR Training blog

Blog.hsoi.com John Daub's blog

Made in the USA
Monee, IL
21 September 2023

43087664R00141